Trapped in Tunisia, Troubled by Bears, & Other Events

by
John Robertson

Library and Archives Canada Cataloguing in Publication

Robertson, John, 1921 -
    Trapped in Tunisia, troubled by bears and other events / John Robertson.

Short stories.
ISBN 978-1-896238-13-5

    I. Title.

PS8635.O22856T72 2012   C813'.6   C2012-902501-1

TWIN EAGLES PUBLISHING

Box 2031
Sechelt BC
V0N 3A0
pblakey@telus.net
604 885 7503

twineaglespublishing.webs.com

CONTENTS

Part 1

TRAPPED IN TUNISIA

When the editor of Canada's Legion Magazine suggested that I produce a memoir on the air war in the Mediterranean, I wrongly assumed that he was interested in fiction. The story I produced, *Dressed For Battle*, was therefore based on my own experience but credited to the fictitious Ferret Plumley.

Dressed For Battle was well enough received to lead to a series of reminiscences which also covered my stay in Malta. But do not be surprised if you are suddenly transported to the Algerian Sahara Desert where I spent a year imprisoned by barbed wire as the guest of the Vichy French.

And please do not be nonplussed by references to "Swordfish." The Swordfish was (and still is in many museums) a pre-WW2 open cockpit biplane known facetiously as the *Stringbag*, because of its strut and fabric construction. However, it has the distinction of sinking more enemy shipping than any other type of allied aircraft.

Freddie Nottingham and I usually flew together; he the pilot, I the observer. The pilot was usually referred to as the Driver, while my job was to do the navigation, operate the radio and communicate in morse code. Malta is a small island remote from everywhere. Getting home safely from a night operation was always my major concern, so navigation was the most important of my duties.

Another important duty did materialize on one occasion, and it led to the story of *The Red Handle*. The stories that follow are all based on similar adventures.

After my release from captivity I was involved in the Pacific Theatre, where the enemy liked to indulge in suicide attacks on our ships. *Kamikaze* is the story of one such attack.

DRESSED FOR BATTLE

Walter Gzinsky was a Prairie boy. He had volunteered for the Navy because there was no appeal in footslogging in the Army. And he'd volunteered for flying duty because flying seemed like a glamourous occupation. But after three months of flying from an aircraft carrier in Mediterranean winter storms, volunteering for anything at all was beginning to lose its glamour.

Walter was a young man of twenty one. Handsome in a rugged sort of way, he found a ready wit and a Naval Officer's uniform with pilot's wings a considerable advantage in his off duty activities, most of which involved removing the uniform at some stage of the evening.

Early in 1941, the Fleet was based in Alexandria, waiting for the Italians to put to sea. Part of the time the Fleet spent in harbour refuelling, which was what Walter enjoyed doing at the Hotel Cecil. But when they were at sea, Walter's monotonous daily routine involved climbing resentfully into the front seat of an aircraft before even the sun was awake, searching the angry grey sea in case the Italians had ventured out, coming down for breakfast, and then taking off again on a fruitless anti-submarine patrol, all the time hoping his observer could navigate home and the aircraft carrier would be where it was supposed to be by the time he got there.

Even the weather was monotonous. Day after day high winds ripped the clouds into flying mist while curtains of rain beat down the white caps into angry slicks. The only unpredictable was whether they could actually take off with the flight deck ahead of them pitching fifty feet up and down with every sea, and whether they could see anything if they did get airborne; or whether they would get ready to fly off only to be stood down and go back to finish their disturbed night's sleep.

It seems unlikely that Walter was the only one in the squadron to get lazy. But he was certainly the only one to be caught out.

He resented being rolled out of his hammock knowing he would probably be rolling back thirty minutes later. So he got into the habit of pulling on his uniform over his pyjamas so that he could quickly strip off again and climb straight back into his hammock before it had time to get cold. If they actually had to take off he could don his life jacket over his uniform and he was dressed for battle.

He scorned to wear a flying suit unless it was actually snowing. That worked well until the twenty eighth of March, when the monotony suddenly ceased.

The Admiral had been waiting so long for the Italians to put to sea that he eventually became impatient. He decided to put out some ground bait in the form of a pair of unprotected convoys, while the battle fleet pretended to lie innocently at anchor back in Alexandria. When an RAF reconnaissance aircraft sent out a sighting report he knew the bait had been taken.

He could have sailed at once, but Alexandria was a nest of spies and news of the Fleet sailing would have reached the enemy before the Fleet did, and the Italians would already have left for home. So the Admiral postponed sailing till after dark. And just for good measure he added a little touch of his own.

Japan, which had not been invited to join the war at that time, maintained a consul in Alexandria, a gentleman with an oversized posterior who was generally known as the Blunt End of the Axis. Everyone knew he was reporting regularly to the Germans and Italians on the British Fleet movements. Most of his afternoons were spent on the golf course, so the Admiral went ashore with his golf clubs and his overnight bag, challenged the Blunt End, and played a reasonably relaxed round of golf. As soon as it was dark he picked up his bag, returned to the flagship, and the fleet slipped quietly away.

Of course, the next morning was as bleak and foul as ever, with the usual low cloud and mist and rain so that not even the seagulls could see the bows of the ship from the bridge. But this day there was a real quarry to search for. The aircraft carrier mounted a dawn search which actually got airborne, and A-for-Ashcan was on the left edge of the search with Sub-Lieutenant Ferret Plumley navigating and Leading Airman Gordie Hall as the telegraphist-air-gunner.

It was when they were disgustedly giving up all hope of seeing anything through the cloud and rain that Walter saw a swirling black smoke cloud that was fast disappearing into the fog behind them. In Walter's book black smoke clouds meant exploding anti-aircraft shells. And if someone was shooting at them it could only be the enemy.

This could be the big moment of their naval careers, the moment all their training had been focused on. Ferret's job was to code up a sighting report, telling the Admiral which ships they had found and exactly where they were. Gordie's job was to tap it out on the Morse key. And it was up to Walter to keep the enemy in sight till the attack squadron arrived.

But as the clouds swirled about them Walter could feel the panic building up inside him. He couldn't even see the enemy, and he might well lose it before Ferret could report it. They hadn't been able to see what ships they were or which way they were heading. Then a yell from Gordie through the voice-pipe brought him craning out through the open window, the slipstream trying to tear the goggles from his helmet. There they were, just five hundred feet below, at least two battleships and several destroyers, guns flashing wickedly and yet seeming so puny, like models in a toy-shop window.

In a moment they were lost again below the clouds. Walter put the nose down in a diving turn that brought Gordie slithering forward to join Ferrer in a heap against the bulkhead. There was no hope of surprising the enemy now, so the most important thing was to find them again and verify their course and speed. At two hundred feet they fell out of the cloud, and there was the enemy steering towards them, suddenly sharply visible against the dark background of the sea.

While Walter turned away to increase the range Ferret checked their position on the chart-board and coded up a sighting report for Gordie to send. But suddenly the sky was appallingly bright, and then instantly horribly black, as a shell exploded close ahead and they flew into the cloud of smoke and glowing shell fragments. A-for-Ashcan flipped over on her back. Arrows of hot metal ripped through the fabric of the wings.

Ferret and Gordie hung impotently upside down by their monkey straps until they knew for a certainty that Walter was dead and the aircraft was on fire and they would never send their historic sighting report.

But Walter was not dead, and the Ashcan was not on fire; though by the time they were right way up again hot oil was spraying back into the cockpit. Ferret retrieved his chart-board from the debris at his feet, Gordie sent out a few preliminary burps with his Morse key to make sure the radio was still functioning, and the signal was sent.

Walter's helmet had become detached from the main voice pipe. By the time he had realised he was disconnected and struggled with the oily tubes to plug himself back in Ferret was yelling from the back. "This some new manoeuvre you're trying out? Give us a bit more warning next time." It was good to hear his Newfie nonsense coming down the tube.

"Got to keep you loafers in the back awake somehow," Walter said. "I've got problems in front here. Bloody oil pipe's leaking. I'm going to have to wrap my scarf round it." The large square of silk, pale blue with a hundred and fifty six golden nudes, was Walter's good luck talisman. He never flew on operations without it.

"We're still alive so I suppose you're still with me little darlings," he muttered as he stuffed his treasure into the oily spray.

He found the voice pipe with his mouth. "This motor won't last long, it's running rough already. How far back to the ship?"

"About ninety miles," Ferret told him.

"How far to the African coast?"

"About the same."

"Then we'll head south for the coast. I'd rather try to find Africa in this muck than a floating tin can. Especially with your navigation."

So while they limped hopefully through the scudding rain clouds the torpedo bombers made their attack and the battle developed without them. In just over an hour they landed in the Western Desert, where an army tank mechanic made some rudimentary repairs and replaced their lost oil.

"Much obliged to you," Walter said, "but don't talk about this, will you? If Their Lordships find out these things keep running without oil they'll expect us to do it all the time."

The uniform Walter had been so proud of was soaked with oil. Oil oozed from the sleeve of his jacket and re-lubricated his hand every time he wiped it clean. The legs of his pants hung slimy and sodden. Disgustedly he undressed, and flung pants and jacket down onto the desert sand.

"Nice line in flying gear!" Ferret observed as Walter's brightly striped pyjamas came into view. "Egyptian Navy issue?"

They raided a deserted fuel dump for enough four gallon cans to refuel the Ashcan, and during the next two days they made their way back across the desert in short hops, refuelling where they could. Wherever they landed, the apparent Navy habit of flying in striped pyjamas excited interested comment.

When the battle fleet returned triumphantly to Alexandria the three of them were there to watch it enter harbour. They had no idea what had happened, but there could be little doubt. The fleet was in line ahead formation. The sirens of the capital ships were whoop-whooping in the way that no other sirens in the world can sound. The gyro stabilisers of the destroyers had been connected in reverse so that the small ships rolled from side to side like a gaggle of waddling geese. The fleet was in a joyful mood. They had inflicted heavy losses on the Italian fleet.

But one casualty that was never mentioned in the official despatches was the dignity of Walter Gzinsky, who had to report aboard amid all the celebrations wearing a Navy cap and striped pyjamas.

THE RED HANDLE

It had been a depressingly uneventful day. Even from a height of five thousand feet we had seen nothing to break the boring vista of untroubled Mediterranean below us, certainly not the small fishing smack we had been searching for. We had climbed in the clear morning air till we could see as far as the coast of Tunisia and we had dived down to clip the wave tops in case there was something we had missed. But it seemed no-one was out on the water that fine September morning.

The Intelligence people in Malta had called for a search aircraft to locate a party of Free French who were supposed to be escaping from Tunisia in a small boat. It was 1941 and there were Hurricanes and Wellingtons and Marylands and Sunderlands available on the island. But it was usually the Swordfish that took on such odd jobs. The Swordfish was slow, certainly, but a biplane was eminently suited for such work. The cockpit was open so that I could lean over the side and get an unobstructed view through my binoculars. And the slipstream at slow speeds was not particularly uncomfortable.

It had been a depressingly uneventful day, and Freddy Nottingham was just commenting acidly that the Intelligence people had probably got the month wrong when I noticed something that dispelled the boredom as fast as a skunk at a wedding.

I picked up the voice pipe. I needed to shout for Nottingham to hear me over the engine noise, but I didn't want him to think I was panicking. "Freddy, I think we'd better start heading back."

His South African voice was thin in my helmet. "The bar won't be open for another two hours. What's the panic?"

"No panic," I shouted back hurriedly. Not yet, anyway. "But have a look at the red handle on the port side."

Nottingham's language at the best of times was the ripest in the squadron so I waited for the speaking tube to burst into flames. He looked over the side for a long time. And then I knew he was really worried. "We do seem to have a small problem," he said.

I had never paid much attention to the red handle in the past. It was one of those things that were always there, something for the ground crew to use, obviously important but not something you were concerned with in the air. It was an oval ring of steel large enough for a man to grip with one hand. It was attached to a foot long lever pivoted at the bottom of the strut that connected the inboard ends of the upper and lower mainplanes. And of course it was painted red. When the handle was pushed down it locked the wings into place after they had been unfolded. (Carrier borne aircraft need to have folding wings for stowage in the hangar below the flight deck.)

Nottingham's 'small problem' was simply that the red handle on the port side was sticking out horizontally instead of fitting snugly down against the strut. Possibly it had never been pushed properly into place before we took off. Possibly the vibration had caused it to lift out of place. The one thing we knew was that the red handle was not where it should be and the pins locking the wings in place must already be halfway out. Possibly more than halfway. And if the vibration had lifted the handle this far it could just as easily lift it the rest of the way. More easily perhaps.

Nottingham was already turning the Swordfish homeward, turning to port to ease the strain on the port wing. And turning very gently. "We can pile the coal on and belt like hell for home and hope we get there before the wings fall off," he shouted, "or we can throttle back and reduce the vibration and start praying they haven't greased the locking pins. What's your preference?"

If the two wings on the port side suddenly folded back with a ninety knot slipstream to help them we would roll over a few times and plummet untidily into the sea. Fast. And break into small pieces. But before that happened one or other of the wings would have sliced through my rear cockpit and severed me into at least two pieces. I had no interest in either of Nottingham's alternatives. I started to explain my problem.

Nottingham was in no mood to listen. "This isn't a bloody debating society. We've got to do something right now."

"Then bail out," I suggested. "I'd rather die swimming than be chopped liver."

"We can't bail out, we're too low. And climbing's going to strain the wings more."

I had an idea. "If we put more strain on the wings won't the locks press against the pins and hold them in place?"

"Good thinking. We'll climb."

We climbed, and I busied myself with the Morse key explaining to Malta why we might be late home. Very late.

Then I stared out at the red handle, willing it to stay where it was, leaning hard against the side of the cockpit in the vague hope of reducing the vibration, invoking the power of positive thinking and picturing it slipping back down where it belonged. Anything but thinking about what might happen if the wings slammed back.

Nottingham was shouting again. "Is there anything back there you can break off?"

"What for?"

"You might be able to lean out and push the bloody handle down with it."

"I'm no acrobat," I said. "I might as well get out there and push it down with my foot."

Nottingham was silent. Then, "Why not?"

"Why not what?"

"Get out there and stand on it."

I must have been near to panic by then or I would have told him to stick his ridiculous suggestions in some impossible place. Instead I reached for the parachute where it was stowed against the bulkhead and clipped it on the front of my harness. There were toe holes in the side of the fuselage and I had used them often enough to climb in and out of the aircraft. I had even used them to climb forward and stand on the wing beside Nottingham. But that had been on the ground. Without a gale blowing back from the propellor.

And without the heavy bulk of the parachute projecting from my chest like a grotesque hump. I pictured the slipstream wrenching my fingers loose from the side of the aircraft and sending me tumbling into space. And then I pictured the wing smashing back and turning me into hamburger. After all, I had been suggesting bailing out.

At the worst I would be making an involuntary drop. Anything would be better than hamburger.

Nottingham throttled back to reduce the slipstream and I fumbled with the parachute to make sure I knew which side to find the ripcord. Supposed to count to five and get well clear of the aircraft before pulling the cord, I thought. Not sure I shall be able to wait that long before I panic. Climbing over the side was more difficult than I had expected. The hump on my chest kept my arms apart and threatened to catch on the edge of the cockpit and hang me up. And then, congratulating myself on being able to cling like a fly to the outside, I found I had forgotten to disconnect my wireless cable and speaking tube and I was still tethered to my cockpit. There was no way I was going to climb back in to rip them out, so with one hand I tore off my goggles and helmet and let them drop back into the cockpit. And I found I was as good as blind unless I kept my head down or faced aft to keep my eyes out of the direct wind.

Edging my way forward fumbling for the toe holes was not such a problem as I had expected. I had done it be-fore. I knew the way. I can remember no fear of falling once I was over the side, just a fear of getting to the red handle too late. When I reached the wing beside Nottingham he reached out and held me with his left hand, and I remember making a desperate lunge for the vertical strut two feet out along the wing and clinging to it with both arms.

I have never stamped on a scorpion in the desert with such satisfaction as I stamped on that red handle. It went down easily and I kicked it several times to make sure it was home. And then I realised I was standing two feet away from the fuselage and I had to get back. That was when the reaction set in and I started to shake. So I have no memory of the return trip. I remember falling into the cockpit and unclipping my parachute and putting on my helmet and wondering if they would charge me for the goggles that had blown away. And when I put on my helmet Nottingham's voice was competing with the Morse on the wireless and I recognised my call sign.

Malta must have been calling for some time. They had some useful advice. Pulling the red handle up to the horizontal position only freed the handle. The locking pins were still in place. They could only be withdrawn by forcibly lifting the red handle all the way.

We decided not to mention my extra-vehicular expedition. Fooling about like that could be a court-martial offence.

THE BIG ONE

Brady Harmon had never felt so good. He was twenty years old, young enough so that everything seemed good, and good looking enough to attract more of the Maltese ladies than he could cope with. There was glamour in being overseas, even being in the war.

And particularly in being an observer in an operational squadron. And there was exhilaration in the sick fear in his guts every time he took off in the dark to attack a convoy, wondering whether he would ever see Malta again.

Brady's job in Malta was to sink as many enemy ships as he could before they reached North Africa with supplies for General Rommel. And he enjoyed it. Not from any sense of patriotism or dedication, but because of the excitement, the illusion of personal superiority. And because he was too young to know better. The ethics of sinking shiploads of soldiers, or even sinking ships at all, were far beyond his horizon. His moral dilemmas had so far mainly concerned the young ladies he met in Maxims on the nights when there was no flying. So it came as a shock when he found himself forced to make the greatest decision of his life one dark night two hundred kilometres from home.

It was well past noon, and the lizards were baking themselves in the sun on top of the loose stone wall that bordered the airfield. The Malta hillside to the north was terraced with similar walls, walls that had been in place for centuries to contain the groves of olive trees. Closer at hand were the reminders of war, the squadron office reduced to a heap of rubble, the sad black skeletons of burned out aircraft lying twisted and grotesque among the fig trees.

The figs were ripe and warm in the afternoon sun, and Brady's daily routine included stopping in the deserted monastery garden to pick his fill on the way to inspect his aircraft. This time a messenger interrupted his browsing.

"The CO wants to see you, sir. Right away."

When he arrived at the converted ammunition block-house that had become the squadron office, Chuck Gautier was already there. Chuck was his pilot, a French Canadian with red hair and a permanent freckled grin and a broken nose left over from an argument in a Port Said bar. As Brady liked to tell the ladies in Maxims, "He sits in the front seat and does the driving."

"It's a special job," the Commanding Officer said. "A ten thousand ton ammunition ship. I thought you two would want first crack at volunteering."

This presented no decision making problem for Brady or Chuck. It was not a matter of heroism. Sinking an ammunition ship simply promised to produce a more spectacular bang than usual, and since making bangs was what life in Malta was all about it seemed only sensible to be at the head of the queue for the Big One. They volunteered.

"It's just left Syracuse," the CO said. "An Intelligence contact says it's fully loaded with tanks as well as ammunition."

Finding the ship would pose no problem, even in

the blackness of a moonless night. The Italians always ran their supplies during the non-moon part of the month, but the squadron had been newly equipped with a radar system that enabled them to surprise the enemy even on the darkest nights. And anyway the convoy route was worn into Brady's chart board by constant repetition, so if the ship had left soon after dark and maintained the usual course and speed he knew exactly where to find her.

Once airborne, after the first brief exchange of pleasantries Gautier and Brady were silent for a time. Shouting into the rubber mouthpiece of a speaking tube over the noise of the engine in an open cockpit was tiring. So was trying to understand the replies that filtered dimly back. The ritual of setting course had been established many months before.

"Everything alright in the back?"

"Eh?"

"Everything alright, I said."

"Pretty cold." Brady was always pretty cold at night in the back seat, and Chuck knew it. But it paid to keep reminding him.

"I suppose it wouldn't be any use asking you for a course to steer?"

"Quite right. Keep on climbing for a bit and I'll work on it."

He gave Chuck the course to intercept the target's expected position, and settled down to a couple of hours' boredom in the lonely blackness. From time to time he checked the radar screen. Eventually he was rewarded by a faint blip at the top of the green trace that shone so brightly in the dark cockpit.

"Something about twenty miles ahead," Brady announced with some satisfaction. "Dead ahead. She's right on schedule."

"Just as well. The weather's closing in. I'd hate to have to find her without your magic box."

Cocooned in the enveloping engine noise, his face pressed against the rubber mask of the radar screen, Brady could lose all sense of height or speed or cold or fear. Nothing else existed but the flickering green echo, the need to keep it on the centre line, the feeling that it was the blip itself that was the enemy to be attacked.

Gautier's voice brought him back to reality. "She's right ahead of us. There's a gap in the clouds. But she's lit up like a bloody Christmas tree. Have a look at her through the glasses."

Brady looked ahead through the blurring arc of the propeller and the mist and the rain. She looked more like a cruise ship ablaze with lights. Only, as Gautier put it later, "Even the Eyeties don't hardly run cruise ships in the Med, not in wartime."

"The last time I saw anything like this it was a hospital ship," Brady yelled back. "There should be a bunch of escorts with her, do you see any?"

"Not yet, not till we get a bit closer. You get anything else on the box?"

"Not a damn thing in the whole area. Let's get closer."

So they waited impatiently, and as they closed they

went over all the possibilities.

"Are you positive Intelligence didn't have any other ships leaving? You could have got it wrong." Tact was not one of Gautier's strong points.

"They didn't have anyone else leaving, or ready to leave, or anyone else in the whole bloody ocean, let alone a cruise ship or a hospital ship or even a Christmas tree. And just in case you were about to ask, yes I'm quite sure my navigation's right, I've double-checked it three times over."

"Get on the blower and get someone to wake up those idiots at Intelligence."

"Wireless silence in force on all these trips, you know that. Anyway we wouldn't get a reply. We're on our own."

Soon there was no doubt at all. The ship was close enough to open fire on them, but it didn't. There were large red crosses painted on the covers of the cargo hatches. The whole thing blazed as brightly as a cocktail party on the lawn at Government House.

And as they circled closer at five hundred feet, "There's some cheeky bastard actually waving at us," Gautier yelled indignantly.

They circled again, less to look at the ship than to give themselves time to think.

Intelligence said it was an ammunition ship. What they saw was a hospital ship. It could be genuine, or it could be an ammunition ship disguised.

They had been ordered to sink it, but it was unthinkable to sink a hospital ship. Was it worse to let a shipload of ammunition get through to the enemy and possibly kill allied troops, or was it worse to break international law and kill non-combatant medical personnel?

They argued and they compromised, they changed their minds and changed their minds back again, and they cursed the Italians and they cursed the Intelligence people. They finally persuaded themselves the weight of Intelligence and Photo Interpretation was in favour of its being an ammunition ship in disguise. And then Gautier clinched it.

"What's she doing so low in the water? She must be loaded down with something. You think it's medical supplies?"

Brady didn't. It was time to make the decision, the first major decision Brady had ever faced.

It was the easiest attack they had ever made. There was no gunfire to put them off. They could run in as close as they wished before releasing the torpedo. The ship took evasive action, but too late to have any effect.

Perhaps the torpedo was a dud. Perhaps Charles Gautier's heart wasn't in it and he hadn't aimed too carefully. But there was no tell-tale surge of smoke from the ship's funnel, no flash of flame, no tremendous explosion of ammunition. The enemy sailed serenely on.

For the next few days and nights Malta was beset by air-raids, so they had other things to think about. And then came the night when Brady Harman was shot down in flames. He had made the most momentous decision of his life, but he would never know whether it was the right one.

THE MALTA FERRY

It was Colonel Benskin who gave it the name. "We'll call it the Malta Ferry," he said, "You fellows have got yourselves a steady job." We were in his office in the Malta military headquarters, a cavernous warren cut deep into the rock of historic St. Angelo castle in Valetta. Colonel Benskin was Head of Intelligence. It was the summer of 1941.

Lieutenant Charles Lamb and I had become involved in Benskin's clandestine operations by accident. We normally flew together in a Swordfish of 830 Fleet Air Arm Squadron, attacking enemy shipping and shore bases. Lamb was the pilot and I was the observer, or navigator. The Swordfish was an obsolescent open cockpit biplane. Obsolescent, but it eventually proved to have sunk more shipping than any other allied aircraft in WW2. We happened to be with our Commanding Officer in his office on the bomb scarred airfield of RAF Halfar when he received a phone call from the Colonel asking for the loan of an aircraft and crew. It sounded as if something exciting might be brewing, so we naturally volunteered for the job. We were young, and not yet experienced enough to stay out of trouble.

As we arrived at St. Angelo, the sirens were warning of the inevitable air attack, and we were happy to be welcomed to the safety of thirty metres of rock overhead. Colonel Benskin introduced us to the Air Commodore commanding the island's air forces and the Rear Admiral responsible for Naval operations, so it seemed evident that something high level was afoot. The job turned out to be a return trip to the coast of Tunisia, delivering two secret agents and rescuing one who was on the run. Not particularly dangerous, but at least something urgent. Of all the aircraft on the island, a Swordfish had been selected because of its short take-off and landing run. And we were expected to land on a small dried up lagoon near the beach.

We spent an hour discussing the problems. The trip to Tunisia and back was beyond the range of the Swordfish. For such long trips we normally carried a massive barrel shaped long range tank in the observer's cockpit and moved the observer back into the Air Gunner's place, but in this case there would not be room for Benskin's two agents as well as me. We eventually decided to leave the long range tank and the observer's seat and the radio and the Lewis gun behind, and stack just enough four gallon cans of fuel for the return trip around the three of us once we were standing in place. Not comfortable, but we had nothing better to offer. Once on the ground in Tunisia, our passengers would have to run for it while Lamb and I refueled the plane from the cans. It seemed a reasonable solution. Until Benskin remembered to tell us the passenger we were picking up might have a posse of gendarmerie close behind. And even German SS.

At this point he unlocked a cabinet and took out two Mauser pistols, which of course he made us sign for. We didn't think at that point to enquire about the legality of shooting at the police of a neutral country.

Our landing site was to be about a hundred miles south of Sousse in a deserted area occupied only by a few

Arab fishermen. Our arrival was to be timed for first light so that we could distinguish the place but not attract much attention from early risers. This seemed to offer no problem, because Lamb and I were used to making a close timed and accurate arrival on targets.

We were given a password for the man we were to pick up. He was to identify himself as "Moselle" or he would be an imposter. We were given a wad of Tunisian money, which also had to be signed for, and the phone number of a man named Jacques for use in case anything went wrong. We didn't know how to use a Tunisian pay phone, and anyway it was hardly likely to accept paper money, but Lamb and I were too enthralled by the adventure to think that far ahead. We learned a little about the intelligence community in Tunisia, but not enough to be of use to the Germans, if we should be persuaded to talk. (This sounded ominous.) Benskin explained that there were several different rings of agents involved, none knowing the identities of the others. Their job was to prepare the country for Rommel's eventual advance into Tunisia.

Tunisia at that time was a colony of France, unlike neighboring Algeria which was an actual Department of France. The Tunisians were therefore apparently fairly sympathetic to the British, while the Algerians were as antagonistic as the French because they considered the British had left them in the lurch at Dunkirk. But both countries were controlled by German overlords, and it was these we should be careful of.

We returned to Halfar full of plans and high spirits. The airfield had been attacked again while we were away and the work crews were busy levelling the surface. There were no runways to be repaired because our Swordfish and the RAF Hurricanes were expected to fly from any surface. Our aircraft was well hidden among olive trees in a deserted monastery garden, so it had suffered no damage. We set to work stripping the unnecessary equipment out of the rear cockpits, and arranged for twenty-five four-gallon cans to be brought from the fuel dump later that night. The whole operation was to be so hush-hush that we planned to make most of the preparations ourselves after dark.

Shortly after midnight we were wakened by the mess steward. "Charlie Orange want you in Officers' Mess," he told us. (Charlie Orange was the phonetic extension of CO, which stood for Commanding Officer, and the Maltese found it very funny.) "Lots of people there, and sandwiches," he added. We hastened to the Mess, hungry for sandwiches since we had missed the usual pre-operation meal. The steward was certainly right. The small room which served as a Mess seemed full of people, and there were indeed sandwiches, the latter fast disappearing into the former. The Air Commodore was there, and the Rear Admiral, and Colonel Benskin, and two army officers we assumed were his aides, and our CO. And two men in windbreaker jackets, one tall and thin and the other short and tubby. Benskin introduced us and we shook hands with our passengers for the night. I had been wondering what a secret agent would look like. These two looked like a music hall double act. (We learned later—very much later—that they were captains of Tunisian industry, as influential as any men in the country.)

Down on the airfield my usual pre-operation stomach cramps and tenseness were competing with the urge to giggle as we strapped in our two music hall actors, and the ground crew stacked cans of fuel around us. Our passengers appeared nonplussed, evidently not expecting to be standing uncomfortably with their upper halves exposed to the wind in what must have appeared to be a relic from a WW1 movie. We checked that Lamb had the all-important tool to open the fuel cans, and we waited in the silent darkness until the time for take-off.

I could guarantee an accurate landfall, even with varying winds, because of the box of small canvas bags that accompanied my chartboard. The bags were usually contained for safety in sealed cans, but on this trip there had not been room for the cans.

Once airborn, I would unplug the mouth of one of the bags and drop it over the side. When the water reached the enclosed sodium, the chemical would burst into flame and burn fiercely, long enough for me to take a number of compass bearings on the receding light. The bearings told me the exact track we were making good, and I was able to instruct Lamb on changes of course to steer.

As we approached the Tunisian coast we were relieved to be able to distinguish the dried up lagoon that was to be our landing ground. Lamb skipped the customary precautionary circuit, and suddenly the engine's roar became a sigh as we started to lose height. With a final burst of engine Lamb put the Swordfish down on the sand, and I helped our passengers to unfasten their safety belts, and instructed them in bad French to scramble out as soon as I gave them the word. Lamb was used to landing in confined spaces after operations in Greece, so we came to a stop well before the saucer-shaped depression ended. There was a clatter of collapsing cans as the two men scrambled clear of their confinement and disappeared over the side of the aircraft. And that was the last we saw of them. I gave Lamb the all clear, and there was a roar I felt must have been heard in Tunis as he turned the Swordfish ready for an emergency take-off.

And then the sense of drama began. We could not yet see far in the early light, and there could well be a hostile posse descending on us from beyond the dunes. A figure appeared through the mist, and I remembered the gun at my belt. Feeling like Errol Flynn I pulled it out of its holster and presented it over the side at the approaching man.

"Le passe-mot," I yelled dramatically, forgetting that he could hear nothing over the noise of the engine still ticking over. The man ran right up to the Swordfish, shouting something I couldn't hear, ran right up to where the gun was pointing at him and yelled

"Moselle, Moselle." And as I put the gun away I started to laugh. I was a mere twenty years old, not long out of school, I had never before handled a handgun, and a man was letting me point a pistol at his head. And then I laughed harder, because I remembered I had forgotten to release the safety catch.

But I had urgent work to do. I yelled. "Attendez!" and began dropping heavy cans over the side while Moselle waited, dumbfounded. Lamb was jumping to the ground from the lower wing ready to open the cans, and I decided it would save time if Moselle heaved out the cans for us while I started the refueling process. I jumped out, and over the engine noise explained in school French and with gestures what I wanted, and showed him where the toeholds were in the side of the aircraft so that he could climb aboard.

My first job was to stack the opened cans on the lower wing as Lamb handed them up to me. The fuel tank was immediately behind the engine, so next I had to climb up onto the engine Cowling while Lamb took my place on the wing and handed the cans up to me. And then all I had to do was empty the cans into the fuel tank without a funnel, and with the blast from the propellor (a foot behind my head) blowing the fuel over the windshield. It had seemed so easy when we planned it back in Benskin's office in Valetta. It had also seemed exciting, even romantic.

There were two cans left to be emptied when Lamb shouted up to me and pointed across the dunes. In the dim dawn light I saw a small group running toward us. Lamb kicked the two last cans off the wing and heaved himself into the front cockpit. I slid down to the wing and started feeling for toeholds in the fuselage, fumbling my way back past the long range tank. I was still scrambling over the side into my cockpit when Lamb opened the throttle and the Swordfish began to lurch forward across the sand. I heard two gunshots, but we were already airborne and swinging away out to sea.

It was a month and several trips later that Colonel Benskin informed us that there were no more compromised agents to be rescued. But there was one more to be delivered, and he was the most important of them all. Important he may have been, but with a receding chin and an apologetic look and an embarrassed manner he looked more like a country clergyman than a secret agent. In the Navy the chaplain was known variously as the Sky Pilot or Holy Joe. So as Lamb stepped forward to shake the man's hand he was muttering to me, "My gawd, a Holy Joe."

Holy Joe allowed himself to be surrounded by fuel cans without a word. Even as we roped his suitcase to the struts on the lower wing, although he watched the procedure with evident anxiety, he said not a word. When Colonel Benskin had mentioned casually that there was also a suitcase to be delivered we were not amused.

"Luggage is an extra," Lamb announced. "It goes outside on the wing. What's so important about it anyway?" Benskin hesitated. Then, "Two million Tunisian francs," he said. "Take care of it, won't you?"

That had been the first time we were unamused that day. But Benskin had another shoe to drop. "I'm afraid there's another extra to go," he said. "You're dropping him rather far out in the wilds this time, so he'll need a bicycle."

Lamb began to say something. And then he began to laugh, and through the laugh, "Are you sure he's not going on holiday? What about golf clubs?" And soon we were all three laughing uncontrollably.

But the bicycle was not really such a problem. When the squadron moved from one base to another, we habitually carried our own and the ground crews' luggage. The Swordfish would fly uncomplainingly with suitcases, kit bags, and even garden chairs on the wing. And once there had been the CO's motor cycle.

Our landing ground was to be a dried up lake bed a little further inland than usual. When we arrived over it there was plenty of landing room, but the surface had a suspicious sparkle in the early light. I dropped a bag of sodium to see if any water entered the bag to set the sodium flaming. There was no response. We flew low over the area, but the sun was brighter and the sparkle was gone. There were no ripples of water, only an unending whiteness of evaporated salt. It was evidently what it was supposed to be, a dried up lake.

Lamb throttled back and we drifted quietly in for a landing, while I leaned far out over the side to check for anything that might give an indication of water. Lamb cut the engine and we were down. But there was a strange swishing sound and a rattling against the fuselage. And immediately a clanging cascade of heavy fuel cans was erupting from the cockpit and hammering against me as it flew past.

I had no time to think or even wonder what had happened before there was a dreadful silence, broken by a long string of furious curses from below me. I became aware that I was hanging out of the cockpit, dangling from the monkey strap attached to my harness. The plane was up on its nose. Lamb was still cursing, so he was alive. And Holy Joe was missing, shot out of the cockpit with the fuel cans as the tail came up. He must have undone his monkey strap as we came in to land. And then I saw him, ten feet ahead of the aircraft, struggling like a fly in molasses, struggling to extricate himself from the sea of mud below the salt.

I left Lamb to his cursing and eased my way back into the now vertical cockpit. Hanging from its stowage was a coil of rope I always carried, with other unnecessary items, in case of emergency. Holy Joe needed help. He could even drown in the mud. I heaved the rope to him, and he was able to reach out for it. But his hands were thick with slime and when I pulled on the rope it slipped out of his grasp, I had forgotten the elementary precaution of making a noose at the end. That simple operation, with a rope coated with slimy mud, took several minutes. But Holy joe was commendably silent. It was only after he had discovered that the only way to stay afloat was to lie spread-eagled, and I had dragged him to where the wing sat embedded in the salt, that he spoke.

"La valise, s'il vous plait."

I had forgotten the suitcase. And the two million francs. Even the reason why we were stuck in the mud. But Holy Joe, close to drowning, was still intent on his mission. And could still remember to say "Please."

I climbed out onto the trailing edge of the wing to cut the suitcase loose, and lowered it down on the rope to the black bedraggled creature below. Neither of us said a word. My French was not up to coping with a discussion on how he planned to cross a quarter mile of clutching, clinging slime. When he set out for the shore he was a water-spider, walking on the surface of the lake with arms and legs extended. He made progress by sliding the heavy suitcase ahead as far as he could reach, and using it as an anchor to drag himself forward. A slow and laborious progress. I watched him, mesmerized, wondering if that was the way we would have to escape starvation, until Lamb's irate voice in the cold silence woke me.

"Don't drop that rope in the mud, we're going to need it to haul me out of here. My feet are jammed. Otherwise we may have to burn the Swordfish with me in it."

The whole front of the Swordfish, propellor, engine and fuel tank, had been forced back, embedded in mud, mud which was oozing steadily past the broken windshield and dripping down into the cavity where Lamb's feet were imprisoned. A foot further and his whole body would have been entombed. Between us we secured the rope round his legs, and eventually dragged his feet out of his shoes. By that time my hands and arms were coated with mud from the rope, and I had wiped the sweat from my face with my hands. Lamb massaged his legs where the rope had cut in and relaxed, and laughed. "You look as if you're going to sing 'Mammy' any moment."

I wiped his face with one dirty hand and sang a couple of bars, and once again we began to laugh as if we'd never stop.

It was an hour or more before we had lowered down our parachute packs to serve as anchors, and the packet of sandwiches which my steward always prepared for me, and the 'emergency' flask of rum which Lamb always carried, and lowered ourselves gently into the mud, and struggled far enough from the Swordfish to set her on fire safely.

But the signal cartridges we fired into the wreck failed to explode, and she stayed where she was, lonely and useless, until the local Arabs eventually stripped her.

It was several more hours before we finally dragged ourselves onto the shore, chocolate coated ants black against the stark white salt. Holy Joe was nowhere in sight, though his muddy tracks were visible leading into the scrub. We were on our own in a strange country, we looked like scarecrows, we were hungry, and the sandwiches were ruined. Our adventure seemed less exciting than it had when we set out. Even Colonel Benskin's promise to send a seaplane to pluck us off the beach if things went wrong did little to brighten the gloom.

WHAT'S IN A NAME

When I was growing up in England the three commonest names, the names people used if they didn't want to give their real names to the local magistrate or the ticket inspector on the train, were Dick Jones, Jack Robinson and Bill Smith. Presumably somewhere there were real people who belonged to those names, but no-one I knew had ever met them.

In 1941 I was taking a holiday from the war in a French prison camp in the Sahara desert. Why it was French is another story. Before going there (or in case that gives the impression I went there intentionally for a holiday, perhaps I should correct that to 'before being invited to go there by a man with a gun') I was provided with a code which could be incorporated into letters to my loved one.

My loved one, of course, began to notice words and phrases in my correspondence which seemed to have no relevance to either of us. Being of above average intelligence she immediately assumed I was trying to get repatriated on the grounds of insanity. The authorities for whom the messages were intended were not so bright.

They forgot to intercept my letters, and consequently missed several interesting snippets of intelligence which were out of date by the time they finally retrieved them. However, we eventually got ourselves sorted out and developed a fairly chummy relationship. Particularly since the authority concerned always signed himself or herself 'Your loving Aunt Belinda,' assuming apparently that no mere foreigner censoring the letters would have the wit to realise there was no such thing as a real Aunt Belinda.

Life in clink proceeded uneventfully enough until a newly arrived young officer began to take us aside in ones and twos and whisper, "Ssh! I'm from Intelligence." He seemed to have no intelligence to impart and we were presumably expected to say, "Gosh, really?" and ask for his autograph. This behaviour, injected into a group of very bored and slightly dippy people, had only one result. Everyone began taking everyone else aside and whispering, "Ssh! I'm from Intelligence."

New inmates usually arrived in ones and twos as aircraft ran out of fuel or lost their way or were actually shot down by an enemy. There were two exceptions when a destroyer crew and then a whole cruiser load arrived, but they were mere hiccups in the routine.

The next significant event was the arrival of The Three Characters. They were dressed in civilian clothes, if you're prepared to stretch the interpretation of civilian. One was tall and thin, with several days five o'clock shadow, a bald domed head and an aggressive nose. The other two were insignificant beside him, quite young, but there was so little remarkable about them I really don't remember what they looked like.

We gathered round and showered them with questions in the usual way. What's your name? What service? What kind of aircraft? Got any money? Play any poker? The tall one was the spokesman, in a thick Arabic sort of accent. The other two nodded, occasionally saying, "Don't speak

English," in unison as if they'd practised.

If at that time I had known about Larry and His Brother Darryl and His Other Brother Darryl I would have known what names to give them. But I didn't need to name them. They had names of their own. You've guessed? Dick Jones, Jack Robinson and Bill Smith.

We fell about laughing. Later, when we'd recovered a little, someone asked Darryl, "Did you come by ship?"

He smiled, "Yes."

Someone asked the other Darryl, "You in the Army?"

He smiled, "Yes."

Someone asked Larry, "Which one of you was the pilot?"

Larry crossed his arms and pointed at the two Darryls on either side of him and said, "These gentlemen here."

We fell about laughing again. Only it lasted longer. They were as phoney as Tojo's smile, but at least they weren't trying to be anything else.

Throughout the next two days as long as they could answer yes or no we got as many stories from them as we had questions to ask. Their technique was perfect. We couldn't trip them into deviating from their story because they hadn't one.

And then Dick Jones (Larry, remember, the tall one) approached me in the exercise yard, where we did all our private talking because we couldn't be overheard, and said (I swear this is true), "Ssh! I'm from Intelligence."

After I'd fallen about laughing again, and had to be

40

revived, he explained that he'd been given my name because I had a code. And he needed to send some messages home. This, of course, could have been a ploy by some high mucky-muck in the Deuxieme Bureau to get me to admit to unsportsmanlike activities such as having a code in the head and plotting to escape. But he was able to convince me that a distant relative of Aunt Belinda had highly recommended me, so we eventually let our hair down and exchanged ideas. At least I did. It seemed he'd already let his down somewhere else.

What it all boiled down to was that he was a Tunisian Arab on an intelligence gathering mission, the kind of chap who gets paid by the word or the message. And if he didn't get his message home the wife and kids would go hungry. He'd been put ashore, with two naval commandos to operate a rubber raft. Unfortunately no-one had thought to bring along a puncture repair kit and the rubber raft had let them down rather badly some way off shore. They were in pretty bad shape by the time they eventually got ashore, and the locals had to fit them out with whatever clothes they could muster before they dare let the ladies see them.

We got his messages sent away, but only just in time. The next day they came for the three of them and took them away. We never saw them again. We heard via the grape-vine (a scruffy man outside the barbed wire who stuck messages to the under side of the camp dog with band-aids) that they'd been sentenced to long terms in the prison ship in Bizerta harbour.

But every time a newcomer arrived at the camp after

that he brought some item of information useful to the people back home. Somewhere along his route he would have been passed a message from a mysterious gentleman named Dick Jones.

POKER SCHOOL

In my youth I had always thought a poker school was a place where you went to learn to play poker, in the same way that a driving school was a place where you learned to drive or an acting school was where you learned to act. It wasn't until I was in the Navy that I discovered what a poker school really was—simply a dedicated group of people determined to let nothing distract them from the pursuit of the elusive jackpot.

My inauguration into the Longest Poker School In the World occurred late in 1941. I was no expert. But then neither were most of the other forty or so members. I had no money. Neither did anyone else. So the whole seven month long game was conducted on credit, with a complex set of books kept by an ex-accountant and an audit every month so that we could see which of us was set up for life and who was ruined beyond redemption. Because we didn't play for peanuts. The stakes were high, higher than any of us could really afford.

And when I call it a seven month long game, I don't mean we played on and off, whenever we felt like it or whenever it rained. It never rained in the Sahara. I mean that the game went on, day and night, seven days a week, for something approaching five thousand hours; through the Saharan winter, over Christmas, and well into the Saharan spring, though through it all the Saharan sun still blazed relentlessly down. Of course, we didn't all play at the same time. We divided ourselves into six watches—port and starboard for the Navy people, left and right for the Army, and up and down for the Air Force—plus anyone else who felt like dropping in to take a hand. The watches overlapped at times, so the number of players and the faces round the table were constantly changing. Sometimes there might be only three or four people playing. Sometimes there weren't enough seats, and the late comers would have to kneel, complaining about the hard stone floor.

The traffic in and out of the poker room was quite remarkable. No matter what time of the day or night you happened to be looking that way, you could usually see someone either entering or leaving. The Poker School became the major topic of interest. Ordinary conversation became laced with poker terms. Even our pet dalmatian knew Busted Flush meant there were no scraps for supper.

The poker room itself was fairly unremarkable. The walls were limestone blocks, whitewashed from time to time through the years, but still showing in places graffiti from the century of occupation by the Foreign Legion. The once white ceiling, high as it was, showed the dingy blackening of smoke from cigarettes and night-time candles.

The floor was hard and unfriendly, foot-and-a-half square flagstones originally laid level but worn hollow in places by a hundred thousand army boots. The room was where a couple of Army captains slept whenever they weren't playing poker or eating or doing the various things Army captains do. There was very little furniture in the room. Two narrow iron beds, a chest of drawers and a selection of chairs and boxes gathered round the table. And of course the Great Table itself, two trestles placed side by side and covered with blankets that hung down to the floor on all four sides. On the table was the usual litter of cards and cigarette packets and tin lids filled with fag ends. But no money, just mounds of small pebbles gathered from the gravelly ground that the winners scooped in as triumphantly as if they'd been clinking silver.

The traffic in and out of the poker room was bound to excite comment. The Arab guards had become used to it. They watched it every day and every night. At first they had reported it to the Chef de Poste, who reported it to the Commandant de Camp, who sent the Capitaine de Guard to investigate. The Capitaine de Guard was invited to take a hand, and stayed for an hour and lost a whole pile of pebbles, for which he was billed at the end of the month.

From time to time a suspicious Adjutant de Camp paid what he earnestly supposed were surprise visits to check that it really was a poker game and not some subversive activity that went on behind the blue door.

Our captors were French. They had a hundred and fifty of us penned inside the prison camp at Laghouat. Laghouat was an attractive enough little oasis town in the Sahara desert that might have been a great tourist spot in better times. But as POWs we saw little of the town through the barbed wire, so we invented our own diversions. The French had always known the British were mad about games, if not plain mad, so they left us to our poker. The Arabs were mad about games themselves, and on special occasions they were privileged to visit the Salle de Pokeur by invitation. But on those occasions, the best players would happen to be on duty, and French money would miraculously replace the pebbles, and the visitors, playing for cash, would inexplicably lose heavily, leaving behind a great many francs to swell our secret hoard.

So interest in the traffic to and from the poker room died. If boredom prompted one of the guards to switch on a searchlight and illuminate a nocturnal gambler en route, a wave of the hand or an obscene gesture would satisfy his curiosity.

But every two hours the routine round the table would be interrupted. A pair of new arrivals would exchange a few ribald comments with the players, lift the fringe of blanket hanging down and disappear beneath the table. Beneath the table was a square hole in the floor where one of the flagstones had been removed. Beneath the hole was a cellar the exact size of the poker room above it. On one side of the cellar the rock wall had been broken through to make an arched opening about four feet high. In the opening, a half naked man sweated in the light of a flickering butter-filled jam jar, heedless of the noise of the poker game in progress above him, emptying the trolley which he periodically hauled in from the tunnel. And a hundred and eighty feet away another half naked man sweated in the Stygian blackness, chipping at the tunnel face with a worn down bread knife.

POWs have dug a great many tunnels, and this was only one of the many. But we were fortunate in many ways.

We had an empty cellar. It had no entrance, and there was no indication the floor had been disturbed since it was laid a century or so earlier. So our captors knew nothing about it. It gave us a capacious place to dispose of the sand that came out of the tunnel, and somewhere to change our clothes and store our tools. Our starting point was already eight feet below ground, and a gentle slope took us down to twelve feet, at which depth the ground was well compacted and we had no need of shoring against cave-ins. We were digging in sandy gravel that left no muddy tell-tale marks when it was wiped off the body. We had an RAF surveyor who designed the tunnel with a curved self-supporting roof and a four foot height that allowed us to walk through with a fairly comfortable stoop.

We had people knowledgeable in a great many fields; so we had someone able to tear down the electric wiring in our rooms and wire the tunnel with lights set in niches every thirty feet, someone who could make candles out of practically anything that would burn for use after the current was cut off at night, someone who could make us tinder boxes when we ran out of matches, someone who could carve wheels out of firewood for our trolley, someone who could make a theodolite so our surveyor could keep track of our depth underground, and of course someone who could forge official stamps for our counterfeit documents.

I think it was thirty two people who went out the night we opened the tunnel, Americans, Canadians and Brits. Most headed north, where water might be easier to find. My partner Steve Hodsman and I dug ourselves into a sand dune and waited for the inevitable search to die down. One trio actually headed south on an ancient caravan route, naively expecting to trek the eight hundred miles to the Mali border. But the Sahara is an inhospitable place if you're not an Arab and you don't know where the water holes are. The sun is a pitiless enemy, and delirium quickly sets in. And there was a high price on our heads, alive or dead. So we were all back inside within a few days.

Looking back on all those months of poker and planning, I don't think any of us really expected to get clean away. They'd put us down in the Sahara specifically to stop us getting away. But for POWs, escaping is what it was all about; achieving the impossible and getting home if we could, but certainly keeping up our spirits and showing them we could still make a nuisance of ourselves.

I said that we played for high stakes. I suppose we never really believed we'd ever settle up. But when we were released after the invasion of North Africa our accountant produced the books and we paid our debts. After the Longest Poker School in the World the biggest loser was about ten dollars down. There were no big winners—financially speaking. But we were going home. We were all big winners.

CHOCOLATE COATED ANTS

Getting out of gaol had been easy enough. All it required was about six months of steady tunnelling, a few split fingernails and the butter from the Red Cross parcels. The butter, of course, went to make candles, because only things like moles and rabbits like to dig tunnels in the dark.

Getting back home was going to be the problem. Laghouat might have been an oasis paradise to pre-war tourists, but it was several hundred miles south of Algiers in the Sahara desert. The route to freedom lay across the desert to the sea, then across the sea to Gibraltar. An impossible journey, the older and wiser ones said. But to Rollie Harris anything seemed better than stagnating behind barbed wire in a prisoner-of-war camp.

Rollie was in the Army, twenty one years old, over endowed with self-confidence, eager to get back to the war, and even more eager to make himself available to the world's lonely women. Steve Bellman was in the RAF, slightly younger but just as eager. They scrambled silently and grubbily from a hole in the ground just outside the barbed wire one moonless August night in 1942.

The other thirteen teams planned to head north as fast as malnutrition and blowing sand would allow; but Rollie and Steve knew there was no hope the absence of twenty eight bodies could be concealed at morning roll-call, and a hundred mounted Spahi soldiers would be out scouring the desert as soon as they could wake up the horses. So they decided the smart thing to do was go south for a few miles and lie low until the hunt cooled down. Although cooling down was not something that was likely to happen in the late Saharan summer.

By dawn, they were far enough from the oasis that the tall thin tower at the corner of the mosque where the muezzin called the faithful to prayer every day was all they could see above the shimmering horizon. The horizon was shimmering because practically everything shimmered in the Sahara in summer, even at dawn. And after the exertion of crawling a hundred and eighty seven feet through a rabbit hole, and then walking several miles carrying a gallon of water they were beginning to shimmer themselves.

Even though they were actually wearing the water, inside the inflatable Mae West life jackets they'd been allowed to hang onto as part of their uniforms. Their map of the desert water holes was only as reliable as their informant's memory, and their informant was an Arab who had demanded payment by the hole. And they had a long way to go.

In the early light, they saw ahead of them a region of irregular lumpy hillocks, wind-blown dunes quite unlike the miniature rolling hills of the silver screen. The hillocks were sharp topped and lopsided, the sand piled up in a gentle slope on the windward side with an almost vertical face on the leeward side. Rollie called a halt. They dug themselves into the vertical side of one of the dunes, and covered themselves with sand till only their heads were showing. A mounted

Spahi would need a telescope to see them at thirty paces, and the Spahis were not noted for carrying telescopes. It was restful, and Rollie felt he already needed the rest. At last he was free, after months of confinement. And he was gleeful, because HE was smarter than THEY were.

As the sun came up, they were able to see the searchers, a whole troop of Spahis galloping madly and aimlessly about, kicking up the fine sand into miniature dust storms that lifted in the hot rising air till the soldiers and the horses were hidden from view.

As the day wore on, their glee diminished. They had forgotten to bring any kind of headgear, and there was no shade from the practically vertical sun. The supplies in their home-made haversacks were mainly high energy food saved from Red Cross parcels, much of it chocolate; and the chocolate had long since melted to liquid globs.

The conveniently shaped sand dune proved to be the home of a colony of ants the size of silver dollars; and after an advance scout of the ants had located the chocolate and reported back to base, the remainder quickly formed themselves into a militarily precise column and marched across their prostrate forms heading eagerly for the rations. And then a second column rather less militarily precise staggered stickily across their bodies back to home base, laden with most of their high energy diet.

The Spahis criss-crossed the desert all through the day. Presumably they were searching, though from where Rollie lay the operation seemed more like an excuse to exercise the horses. They lay still, and dozed, and wondered if the ants might turn to eating human flesh after all the chocolate was finished. Night came at last, and they were able to dig themselves out and get some exercise and move to a location that seemed less likely to teem with wild life.

The second day was much like the first. The Spahis criss-crossed the desert again, only closer. Another army of ants found them, or perhaps the same colony had simply followed the smell of liquified chocolate. Water in the prison camp had never been particularly fresh, and by this time the portable supply was far from potable. Rollie's head was bursting, his eyes were raw with sand, and it was a toss-up whether thirst was worse than drinking the hot stinking water. Steve muttered and cursed beside him, but Rollie had lost all interest in Steve's problems. He was trying to decide whether freedom was really quite as desirable as he'd been led to believe.

By noon Rollie was hallucinating. He saw rain, and rivers, and bottles of ice cold water. He knew they were hallucinations because his head still pounded and he was still abominably hot and thirsty. And then, suddenly, the hallucinations ceased and the pounding stopped, and he found himself in the old swimming hole nine miles outside Red Deer. It must have been six years at least since he was there. And the last time he was there, the water had been muddy enough to leave a scum on his body, and the water spiders had been skimming around in their thousands.

But on this particular day in 1942, the scenery was different. There was no mud, no water spiders, and the pool was full of cold draught beer. And the beer was gushing deliciously from the mouth of a marble lion ridden by a naked nymph. Rollie was still trying to decide why he was more interested in the beer than the nymph, when three Arab nomads with shotguns stumbled on them and returned them to their owners to claim the reward.

Neither of them was particularly upset. The prospect of nine more days and nights in the desert, and then a long hike through the mountains, had lost its glamour.

It was not until a week or so later that Rollie realised the incongruity of the situation. He wasn't a beer drinker. He wasn't really a drinker at all at that time.

The sequel came years later. He went to see Lawrence of Arabia at the movies. There was one scene where the man who had fallen off his camel staggered exhausted across a wall-to-wall technicolor desert, evidently dying of thirst. It was too much for Rollie. As desperate as the man on the screen, he staggered out of the theatre and across the street to where draught beer flowed out of taps in a tavern.

A SOLITARY QUEEN

Pincher Martin was a Queen. There were a lot of Queens in Laghouat, the oasis paradise in the Sahara where Pincher was a prisoner of war. The Queens were the specialists.

There was the I.D. Queen, a Royal Air Force corporal with a flair for forgery who could produce any kind of identification the authorities might demand, complete with rubber stamp and the appropriate signature. There was the Rag Queen, a Navy tailor who could transform a uniform into a civvy suit overnight. Or a civvy suit into a uniform if necessary. There was the Radio Queen, who kept the clapped out old radio working and faked up dummies for the Camp Commandant to confiscate every time there was a search. And the Code Queen who could use the POW mail to pass useful information received from a contact in the north. The Duff Queen could turn dates and couscous into the most acceptable plum duff, and the Chicken Queen maintained a network of Arabs who were always happy to smuggle in something extra for the pot for a few Red Cross cigarettes.

Time passed slowly for prisoners of war, but as the months went by they became adept at many things. The Rabbit Queen was an engineer commissioned to build airfields for the RAF in the Middle East, but he quickly learned to turn his talents to tunnel building. The Vagabond Queen knew nothing about Show Business but that didn't stop him organising camp concerts, ostensibly for the entertainment of the inmates but quite often to cover a variety of abortive escapes. And of course there was the real live Drag Queen, a sailor who brought his talent with him. And a couple of dresses.

Much of the time they got on each others' nerves, developing petty hates and squabbling about trivialities. And that was when Pincher Martin became a Queen ... the Jankers Queen ... racking up more time in the cells than anyone else. To Pincher, going to cells for fifteen days solitary confinement was like a two-week holiday after teaching school all winter, and easy enough to achieve. He usually threw a few stones at a sentry to get his attention and then told him unpleasant things about his mother.

Pincher would already have his little bag packed with pencil and paper, a few books, soap, toothbrush and toilet paper, and he could be hauled away to the cells within the hour.

The accommodation was not all that impressive, of course. It had been built a century before for the French Foreign Legion. A cell made of limestone blocks, ten feet long by six feet wide, half its length was taken up by a sloping stone slab intended to sleep half a dozen miscreant Arabs or Foreign Legionnaires. Pincher never figured out why the slab was sloping, or why it was raised nearly two feet above floor level. The height was certainly no deterrent to the cockroaches and dung-beetles and scorpions that came happily flocking in within an hour of the great wooden door slamming shut. The facilities were en-suite, with a two foot square doorless cubicle equipped with a well-used metal can that must have been emptied at least once every year.

The walls had been whitewashed many years before. Generations of occupants had left a gallery of graffiti, diaries and portraits, aphorisms and murals, executed more or less crudely in pencil or finger painted in fecal brown. Most concerned activities unlikely to be experienced by POWs, but Pincher was always interested in other people's points of view. He had explored the cells thoroughly many times.

There were several in the block, all more or less identical. The doors were made of two inch thick planks, hanging on huge wrought iron hinges that extended the whole width of the doors and held the planks together. A single two inch thick iron bolt slid into a hole chiselled out of the stone wall to hold the door shut, with a padlock to hold the bolt in place. Small round topped windows closed by heavy iron grills let in air and a little light, but never a direct view of the sun.

It was not a stimulating environment. But Pincher enjoyed writing, thinking and sleeping free from encroachment, and in spite of the stench of the en suite he enjoyed his solitude. There was another advantage to the cells. They were still inside the massive ten foot wall with its ancient loopholes and firing steps for defence against marauding Riffs, but they were at least outside the barbed wire of the prison camp itself.

It is often said that convicts are able to enhance their criminal expertise by learning from the old lags in prison. Pincher had certainly set out to learn all he could from the old lag who shared his dormitory. Peter Reilly was an Army

56

officer who had served his time before WW2 in the Foreign Legion. He knew Algeria, he even knew Laghouat, and he knew a great many Foreign Legion tricks.

He had taught Pincher how an ordinary band-aid, slipped into the space between the door and the frame, could be stuck onto the bolt and used to rotate it. Those huge hinges were bolted to the door with the nuts on the inside of the door; it was no problem to steal a wrench, given time; all the inmates were expert thieves by then. The bars on the windows were no problem according to Peter Reilly. Wrap a towel or a shirt round two bars and twist and tighten like a tourniquet, and the bars would bend steadily and noiselessly. There was always one problem remaining, however. Getting past the guards.

But Reilly had also mentioned something that neither of them had thought important. Pincher was lying on his back one afternoon, watching a chameleon stalk a fly across the ceiling, when he remembered Reilly's words.

"Watch for the dung beetles. They can dig their way right through the ceiling and drop in on you in the middle of the night. The ceilings are only made of laths covered with plaster."

If a mere beetle could dig its way through the ceiling, Pincher reasoned, then certainly a determined POW could do the same. Even without tools. The guards outside would only be watching the door, not the roof. The roof was flat and joined the roof of the guardroom, which in turn actually adjoined the wall next to the main gate.

Pincher decided that dropping from the top of the

wall to the outside seemed like a better bet than bluffing his way past the main gate sentries.

Getting up to the ceiling presented no problem. The corner cubicle was framed in the French equivalent of two-by-fours, a perfect ladder so long as he didn't slip and fall into the reeking can below. Pincher had in his pocket a dinner knife he had brought from the camp. And he had the night ahead.

It was all so easy. As he crawled out onto the roof he was already thinking of a title for the novel he would write when he reached home. But the novel was never to be written. Pincher Martin fell off the edge of the roof in the dark.

KAMIKAZE

It was the First of April. But HMS Indefatigable had been ploughing a furrow back and forth across the Pacific for so many uneventful weeks without putting into port that we were in no mood for playing April Fool tricks. We had been at sea for so long, the Captain had decided to issue the ship's company a daily bottle of beer, just to keep them in practice. And in the evenings they brought a gramophone up to the flight deck and danced. Not a hornpipe or a jig, but two-steps and foxtrots and waltzes. At first they were shy of dancing with each other, but after a few evenings it became a popular pastime. It kept them in practice, in case we ever put into port again.

The British Pacific Fleet has been called The Forgotten Fleet. By April 1945, the war was over back home and the war against Japan was regarded as an American problem. The BPF was a small task force, equipped with outmoded aircraft and supported by a pitifully inadequate fleet of supply ships. With four aircraft carriers, it was the largest fleet the allies had yet assembled, and it seemed impressive enough to us. But we hadn't seen the force the Americans were massing for the final onslaught against the Japanese.

We were a fleet in waiting. We were waiting for orders to join the Americans and share the final victory over Japan. But as the weeks passed, we learned of the political bickering that was excluding us. The Americans would prefer to go it alone and not share the glory, we were told.

However, political perseverance paid off, and the BPF was at last given limited support responsibilities. We moved in till Japanese territory was within striking distance. That, of course, brought us within striking distance of the Japanese Air Force, and at last there was work for our defending fighter aircraft.

Aboard HMS Indefatigable, the defence that 24 Wing contributed to the fleet consisted of two squadrons of Seafires, the seaborne equivalent of the Spitfire. The Spit had certainly been a magnificent aircraft in its day, but five years older and converted to carrier use by the addition of an arrester hook it was makeshift at best. At worst, it was a death trap.

Landing aboard an aircraft carrier entailed touching down on a runway a few hundred feet long, a runway that might be pitching up and down at the time. The Seafire tended to float once the engine was cut, so a landing even a foot too high could result in the hook missing all the arrester wires and the aircraft floating into the safety barrier. Or, worse still, over the side. Even a good landing could end with catastrophe. The Seafire's wheels were too close together for stability; and if a wingtip drooped after touchdown and hit the deck, the aircraft could well spin into the island or over the side. (The island was the carrier's superstructure that housed all the facilities concerned with flying operations, and, of course, the bridge.)

So even before we came within reach of the enemy we had lost more aircraft than the High Command had budgeted. However, pilot morale was high, and when the Japanese bombers began to arrive they suffered heavily. One Seafire pilot even chased his target right through the fleet's defence barrage—and came through unscathed, and then shot the enemy down.

At that time I was an Air Observer. In a multi-seat aircraft the observer could be responsible for any job except the actual driving. Aboard Indefatigable, I was appointed as Wing Observer to 24 Wing, a wing of single seat Seafires that didn't have a seat for an observer. It was not the Admiralty's custom to admit they might have made a mistake, or to look favourably on an officer who phoned up to ask what they thought they were doing. Or even to issue a job description. So I wrote my own.

I suppose I became, in effect, the Wing Nursemaid. I briefed the pilots, made sure they knew their call signs and their codes, marked their location on the silk scarves printed with all the local winds and tides in case they had to ditch, and kept the Ready Room supplied with chocolate bars; and de-briefed them when they came down. I was older than they were, with a full red beard, so they called me Grandpa. There were groups of them taking off and landing throughout the day, so I was kept reasonably busy. And in between times I went up to the Fighter Direction Room to watch the developing air battle on radar, or kept the plot up-to-date in the Operations Room and stood in for the Commander (Ops) while he was on the bridge.

And then came the morning of the First of April. Radar showed an extra large force of enemy aircraft approaching, a larger force than we had so far experienced.

I stood just inside the open door of the Fighter Direction Room, watching the plot develop. Outside the door ran a narrow passage between the Operations Room and the bridge. The Commander (Ops) was with the Captain on the bridge, so I needed to be available in case the Ops Room assistant needed me. The ship's Commander, the second in command, was at his action station as far forward as he could go on the flight-deck, this because he and the Captain must never be casualties of the same bomb.

The Fighter Direction Room was, as usual, hushed and dim, lit only by the bluish glow of the radar screens. We had already donned our anti-flash gear. Even flash from our own big guns could cause major damage to exposed flesh, and flash from an exploding bomb could be fatal. So at action stations we wore a flame-proofed hood that fitted closely over the head and neck and draped loosely over the shoulders and chest. The exposed face was protected by goggles and a removable flap over the mouth and nose. And on the hands we wore loose fitting gauntlets. In the darkened room the white hoods reflecting the blue glow of the radar and the illuminated master plot were all that could be seen. The sailors standing in darkness behind the large vertical perspex plot were marking up the positions of the aircraft; enemy in red, defenders in green. There was an eeriness about the way the coloured marks would appear on the transparent perspex as if by themselves, an eeriness that quickly turned to menace as the plot began to show wave after wave of approaching bombers. The only sound over the hum of the ventilation fans was the quiet voice of the Director passing the Seafires their courses to intercept the enemy, and the acknowledgements coming raucously over the aircraft radios.

As the enemy aircraft closed, I could see gloved hands checking the flaps covering mouths with exaggerated casualness. I hoped the others in the room were as terrified by the strength of the attack as I was. I had been under attack before, but on that occasion I had a gun to keep supplied with ammunition. This time I had nothing to do but watch and wait. I wondered whether the Commander was suffering the same stomach churning fear, watching and waiting by himself at the forward end of the flight-deck without even knowing what to expect.

And then the Japanese attack developed, and the uproar began. We had rapid-fire Oerlikons and pom-poms, and twin four-point-fives that sounded like bombs exploding each time they fired. The ship's hull shuddered and vibrated and everything that wasn't secured fell crashing to the decks. Several times I was certain we must have been hit as a particularly heavy blast seemed to shake the whole ship. My pilots were forgetting their radio discipline in the excitement of the melee that must have been taking place above, and I wished I'd stayed outside to watch the real battle.

Strangely, being actually under attack, hearing the whistle of falling bombs and the scream of the dive bombers, the terror melted away. I felt as I had so many times in the past, when I had been doing the dive-bombing and the enemy flak was flashing past the wingtips and the fear had changed to exhilaration and I was yelling obscenities at them and daring them to touch me.

Suddenly I needed to sneeze. It must have been the material that covered my nose and mouth and made the skin itch. I ripped away the flap and leaned out of the doorway and sneezed. I don't know how many times I sneezed, because in the middle of it there was a frightful explosion that flung me back into the darkened room.

There was no longer any blue glow from the radar. The illuminated plot was dark. There was subdued swearing in the darkness. But the sounds of battle still blared out of the loudspeaker, and I heard the calm voice of the Director handing over control of our fighters to his opposite number in HMS Formidable. Someone removed the blackout screen from the window, and a hazy light streamed in. Outside the window, black smoke was belching up from the flight deck below, and then flames were licking past.

There seemed to be no major damage in the Fighter Direction Room. The blast had thrown me back through the door, so it must have come from the passage outside. I looked carefully out into the passage. There was a roar of escaping steam coming from somewhere nearby, and I guessed the pipe carrying superheated steam up to the ship's siren must have ruptured. Dangerous, but certainly not major damage. I walked along in darkness to the Operations Room, the roar of the steam drowning even the sound of the Seafires' radios. Daylight was filtering in from a jagged space where a part of the Ops Room wall had been, competing with black smoke that smelled horribly of what I hoped would not be burning flesh. In one corner of the room I looked down through a gap in the deck and saw flames at flight-deck level, and the bottom half of a body. Very nearly every wooden cabinet and chart drawer in the Ops Room had been smashed open by the blast, the charts and files and loose paper of every sort flung about the room in a litter over the deck. And then, sprawled over the chart table, I found the Ops Room Assistant. The blood had stopped pouring from his nose and ears, so even in my inexperience I knew he was dead. But I ran back to the Fighter Direction Room to get help, just in case there was any hope for him.

When the explosion below ripped open the hole in the Ops Room deck, the blast must have instantly killed the Assistant and then rushed down the passage toward the bridge. I was suddenly aware how lucky I had been as I sneezed out into the passage. The blast had blown me backwards but I didn't seem to be damaged. The Ops Room was evidently out of commission, so we would have to activate the emergency Ops Room which had been prepared for this eventuality. The Commander (Ops) would want to know, so I made my way along the passage toward the bridge. I had been right about the steam pipe. It ran up beside the companion way which was the main access from the flight-deck to the bridge and every other part of the island. It must have ruptured somewhere below, and scalding steam roared deafeningly up the stairwell and continued up to the next deck where the Admiral's Bridge was located; but it was pouring up with such force that it didn't seem to have time to deviate onto the landing, so I risked it and jumped smartly across to the entrance to the Bridge.

Not much was happening on the Bridge. The Captain

was out on the wing looking down at the flight deck, and reports were coming in on the sound powered telephones. I reported to Commander (Ops), who simply roared with laughter.

He had to shout. "Did you get permission to resume shaving?" (All ranks needed the Captain's permission either to discontinue shaving and grow a beard, or resume shaving and take it off). I felt my face with my hand. No beard, just a rough stubble. My hand came away black.

"Must have been the flash, Sir,"

"You weren't wearing flash gear?"

"Took my mask off to sneeze, Sir."

"Alright. When you get out of this steam trap get back aft and activate the standby Ops Room."

Part of the emergency equipment in the Fighter Direction Room was a rope secured beside the window. By the time I got back there, the fire outside had been extinguished and the Direction staff were evacuating by rope. I followed them down, and for the first time realised we had been hit by a kamikaze. It had crashed on the flight deck right beside the island, blasting the base of the island and destroying the crash barrier support. It had not been an armour piercing bomb, so the flight deck was little damaged. But the main blast of the explosion had been taken by the flight deck sick bay, manned by Ontarian Surgeon Lieutenant Vaughan, who was killed together with one of the Seafire pilots who had reported sick.

The following day the ship's photographer, who had been on deck throughout the whole incident, showed me an eight by ten glossy taken immediately after the kamikaze hit. Debris was still in the air, huge chunks and small pieces, and there was probably dirt on the camera lens. Somehow all had combined to form a shadowy image in front of the exploding aircraft. It was, as clearly as you could wish to see, a small man wearing a parachute harness, grinning broadly and running from the aircraft.

The ghost of the pilot? But why would a kamikaze pilot bother with a parachute?

THE MAD MAJOR

When Steve Prentiss ran away from his home in the Prairies to join the Royal Flying Corps during WW1 the average life expectancy of a pilot was something less than two weeks. They gave him eight hours flying training, pinned on his wings, commissioned him as a Lieutenant and sent him out to France.

Lieutenant Prentiss turned out to be an exceptional pilot. Not an exceptionally good pilot. Just exceptional. There was a popular axiom that only birds and fools flew, and birds didn't fly at night. Lieutenant Prentiss flew by day or by night or any time they'd let him. And quite often when they wouldn't. They grounded him, but still he flew. He flew upside down whenever he could. He flew at treetop height behind the German lines on the assumption that German soldiers were unlikely to be allowed to turn their backs on the enemy and fire behind them. Eventually he took a bullet through the leg and developed a limp that was good for a few beers for many years to come.

He shot down a great many aircraft and a couple of observation balloons, and most of the time he managed to land without breaking anything. So they gave him a medal and they promoted him, and most importantly he came out of WW1 alive. And by that time he was known in all the newspapers as the Mad Major.

Life between the two wars was dull for the Mad Major. He read the newspapers and listened to the radio for any hint of another war. And kept hoping. Like many other returned heroes he found it difficult to get a job. He sold cars, and vacuum cleaners, and insurance, and even burial plots, and then he bought himself an elderly motor coach and fractured the peace of the prairies with a Flying Corps version of a country bus service. The prairie back roads were not much to write home about in those days, but the Mad Major had a schedule to meet. "Had to get those farmers' wives to market and home again," he would say.

"Flew a bit low over the fences sometimes, broke a few eggs." But the farmers' wives loved him and called him 'the dear Major' and invited him home for tea.

Even before WW2 broke out Steve Prentiss was writing begging letters to the Air Ministry. He had been waiting twenty-one years and he was ready for anything. But it seemed the Air Ministry were not that ready for the Mad Major. So he switched to the Admiralty, and the Admiralty finally gave up saying no.

"Their Lordships had kinder hearts than Their Airships," was Steve's verdict.

But even Their Lordships were not altogether generous. Too old for operational flying, they said. They let him put up his wings, but they dropped him down to Lieutenant and they admonished him, "You're not the Mad Major now, or even the Mad Lieutenant."

His first permanent appointment was as Armament Officer at a Naval Air Station in the south of England. By that time they must have sent him on a course, because he was able to teach the trainee fly-boys about bombs and torpedoes and machine guns with an air of authority. To them he was already a middle aged gentleman, slightly portly, with a mane of grey wavy hair and a limp that was always good for a few beers. And a gentle, courteous manner.

When there was an aircraft that needed testing after an inspection or a repair job they let Steve fly it. He managed to get airborne most days, and most of the time he flew right side up. But there was one type of aircraft that was always a challenge to him. The Vickers Supermarine Walrus was an amphibian, a not too elegant boat with four great wings mounted on top, two on each side. And one engine with a pusher propellor that threatened to chop off the air gunner's head if he got excited and bobbed up too suddenly. The Walrus hardly needed a pilot. It wallowed through the air rocking gently from side to side like a boat in a swell. But no-one had ever flown it upside down. And no-one had ever been able to get enough speed out of the Walrus to loop it, or enough courage to risk the wings falling off.

Naturally the Walrus presented a challenge to Steve Prentiss. If no-one had ever looped a Walrus then Steve Prentiss had to do it. But when he did it there was no question of coming back to tell a skeptical audience about it. He did it right over the airfield. And very nearly under it as well. The Mad Major was back. And of course the Mad Major was grounded again.

Every morning as the trainees went out to their aircraft for the daily navigation exercise a very chastened Mad Major was out on the tarmac. He would buttonhole a likely looking pilot. "Got a bit of a hangover this morning?"

he would ask hopefully. "Like me to take her up for you? No bother at all, I assure you." But the Mad Major stayed grounded. And in the afternoon when they went for their armament class there was no gentle, courteous manner. They stripped the Lewis gun blindfolded and put it together again while the Major snarled and barked. The Mad Major was very mad indeed.

Then came the week when the Germans decided to make life uncomfortable for the airfields and radar stations along the south coast of England. Lieutenant Prentiss's Naval Air Station took a royal pasting. A great many buildings were flattened. Some were set on fire. The armament section took a direct hit. But Steve Prentiss stayed lucky. He was putting out a fire in the officers' bar at the time.

The next day, after the tumult and the shooting had died, the Captain and his staff made a tour of the Station to assess the damage. In the distance they could hear a clanging noise like someone hammering an iron pipe. Indeed it was someone hammering, but not an iron pipe. The Mad Major was standing astride an unexploded bomb, belabouring it with a sledge hammer as if he was trying to break it open by brute force.

"Delayed action bomb, Sir," he explained, as if it wasn't obvious, and trying to peel off a salute without interrupting the rhythm of the music. "Very crude things ..." CLANG! "Jerry uses a ..." CLANG! "cheap alarm clock ..." CLANG! "for a timer ..." CLANG! "Easy enough to ..." CLANG! "wreck the mechanism ..." CLANG!

The Captain knew nothing about German bombs,

and as little about Steve's intimacy with them. But he was not about to turn and run in front of his staff. Quietly he dismissed them and suggested they meet him later in his office on the far side of the Station. Then he turned to Steve. He had to shout to make himself heard above the din.

"Lieutenant Prentiss, perhaps you might take a break for lunch about now, and we can discuss the future over a gin."

Steve stopped clanging and knelt down to listen to the thing's internal workings. "It's stopped ticking, Sir," he said.

"I'm not surprised," said the Captain.

"There's another near where you're standing, Sir. How about we fix that one first?" said Steve hopefully.

"Lunch," said the Captain firmly.

Steve Prentiss survived that mad day. He even survived the war. And once again he apparently found it difficult to get a job after the war.

A few years later the Mad Major made the headlines in the national press. He had borrowed an old biplane and flown along the river Thames for a publicity stunt. Lots of people flew along the river Thames, even in biplanes. But the Mad Major had flown UNDERNEATH all the bridges, even the Tower Bridge which has to be raised to let the smallest ships pass. He needed a job, he said. No offer would be refused.

The popular mythology is that the only job offer he got was to ride a motor cycle on the Wall of Death in a circus. He probably took the job. Looping a motor cycle was nothing new. But if it was possible to ride one upside down no doubt Steve Prentiss did it.

2

TROUBLED BY BEARS
AND
OTHER EVENTS

The closest perusal of a British Columbia map will never reveal the location of Jackass Creek. The village, the events recorded in the following stories and the characters involved are all fiction.

I wrote the stories in my own Jackass Creek during a halcyon summer, shaded by a giant grape vine and suitably cooled by appropriate refreshment.

I hope they will give the reader some insight into village life before Facebook and Twitter.

BEARS, BIRDS AND APPLES

It was to be the second most wonderful day of Fran McIntyre's life. The most wonderful, of course, had been Fran's wedding day. But that had been forty six years earlier, and wonderful days had been steadily more rare occurrences in Jackass Creek since then. The hotel and the store and the post office and the streetlights and the tennis courts and the lively community had all passed away as the passenger train traffic had passed away. The tracks still sliced through the middle of the village, but on the east side where the McIntyres lived all that remained were twelve elderly houses and a converted school bus.

Judson McIntyre, standing at the front door in his old blue railway denims, was unaware that this was to be a day unlike other days. To Judson it was enough that it was a brittle September morning, there was probably ice on the highway that threaded the sheer face of the Fraser Canyon the other side of the river, and it was the right sort of day to pick the last of the apples before the late wasps or the early school children got to them.

The Woolworths thermometer that had hung on its nail outside the kitchen window since 1945 said thirty four degrees. Thirty four Fahrenheit, of course, because Celsius had no place in Judson McIntyre's life. Celsius had its uses, Judson would concede, had conceded only the week before in an argument with Tinfish Buckley who owned the hotel and beer parlour on the highway the other side of the river. But

Celsius, like kilograms and litres and seat belts and child-proof plastic bottle caps that only kids could open simply made life more complex for Judson McIntyre.

So, whatever the radio said, it was two degrees above freezing and that meant there was about as much chance of the green tomatoes ripening as of old Art Collins waking up with a blonde in the bed. The year before, the frost had held off in the canyon till December so that those who knew all about the weather were predicting a mild winter, and even the lilacs and raspberries had been fooled into sprouting ready for spring. But then January's arctic high had sucked every last drop of moisture out of the air and forced a frigid creeping tide clear down to Texas, and every sensitive new shoot in the garden had wilted and withered and blackened and the early daffodil leaves had curled up like huge yellow spiders.

The Mcintyres lived in the The Green House On The Hill. The Hill was a bare thirty feet above the hollow below it, and Judson and a crew of teachers from the high school had painted the curling cedar shingles a pale blue the summer before; but it was The Green House On The Hill when Fran and Judson had moved in and Judson had hung the thermometer on the nail forty four years before, and it was a better address than a five figure number on a street that no longer existed. It was a house besieged by a legion of fruit trees and encompassed by an ocean of neatly cultivated vegetable plots. There was no way they could use all the pears and apples and plums and raspberries and peas and three kinds of beans and tomatoes and grapes and spinach and spuds and radishes and kale and cabbage that Judson produced every year; but Judson could no more bear to leave a patch of ground unproductive than he could resist the offer of a cold one on a hot July afternoon.

"Why the sweet san-fairy-ann didn't you go in for farming instead of working on the railroad?" Hillis Usry had asked him one summer evening as they sat on the front steps watching boulders rolling down the bare-scraped canyon face onto the distant highway. Hillis was the school principal, and should have known better. A question like that to Judson McIntyre was an invitation to launch into a five minute monologue. But Hillis had a conversational technique quite foreign to the long term residents of Jackass Creek, whose every thought and utterance and past experience was deemed impressive enough to stop the traffic or at least touch the heart. Hillis liked to ask questions and actually listen to the answers; and seldom volunteered an anecdote or an opinion unless it moved the conversation ahead.

Judson had considered the question for a full five seconds before launching; his long, square chin oscillating slowly from side to side under two days stubble while he considered.

"When war started I was eighteen," he said. "Don't take the time to work out how old that makes me now, I'll tell you, I'm sixty eight. And if I hadn't been so goddam cocky I'd of goldbricked like the others and be living on a disability pension right now. As it is I get nothing from Veterans' Affairs except a new pair of glasses every two years and a free visit to the dentist whether I need it or not. When I came out of the army in forty five I'd had dysentery, malaria, jaundice, Gyppo guts, Malta dog, and my teeth was all rotted away from time in the prison camp. Plenty to qualify for disability, eh? But people back home thought I was a war hero. And I was basking in it, and I was goddamned if I was going to turn down all that free beer just to pretend my guts was shot to hell. You wouldn't believe the way it was in those days, walk into the beer parlour and they was all fighting to see who could pour the most beer down me. Never nothing like it since. More's the pity. I was living with my folks in one of the CPR houses at that time. All but two of them pulled down now. My dad was the roadmaster. Could of finished up as Superintendent but he couldn't take the competition. That's where I get it from, never could argue over anything. Damned if I'd argue over a hundred dollar bill if me and the next guy tripped over it together on the sidewalk. That's why I married Fran. She never got steamed up enough to fog her glasses. She had a quiet little voice in them days, used to trickle out from somewhere up the top of her head like someone had turned down the main steam valve. Anyhoo, there it is. Not much doing in Jackass Creek in them days, not that there is today, but there wasn't no mill then, and you either worked for the CPR or you didn't. So I did. Went right on till I retired."

So there stood Judson McIntyre, trim and spry at sixty eight, five foot ten and a half in his last Christmas slippers, one eye permanently drooping from a collision with a hot cinder, looking out of the front kitchen window that parky September morning. From the bedroom at the back of the house Fran's voice came faintly, calling for him to bring something or other. Fran would call from wherever she happened to be, whenever she happened to think of something worth calling about, seemingly unaware of distance or closed doors or even the enveloping throb of diesel locomotives squatting patiently hour after hour on the tracks a hundred yards behind the house.

Judson ignored her, as he usually did when she was in another room, and watched the traffic crawling along the highway beyond the river. Even this early in the day there was a scattering of campers and mobile homes heading north, but mostly there were logging trucks and semis with trailers grinding wearily up the grade in convoys of six or seven, or coasting down and shattering the morning with the explosive bark of engine brakes reflecting off the bare limestone. Every vehicle had its own distinctive sound, though later in the day when the canyon heated up the distinctions would blur and there would be only the persistent background of what Tinfish Buckley sententiously styled the Ultimate Aural Insult. But the sun was not yet showing over the top of the ridge, would not show for another hour and a half. Until it did the mist would hover above the highway, the dew would remain, the birds would be still, the air would stay crisp and fresh, and the smoke from the burner at the mill would plume purposefully up and away into the cooler air instead of flopping back down to obliterate the valley in the dull blue fog of corporate prosperity.

Fran's voice called again, excited and urgent. "Judson, bring the glasses, quick, there's a bear."

Judson briefly considered whether he could reasonably abandon ship. It was Fran's dearest wish to see a bear, a real bear. Over the years every rock on the steep mountainside beyond the railway line at the back of the house and every tree stump in the monstrous clear-cut desert above the highway at the front had been a bear. But never once had it turned out to be the real thing; and though every tourist and mushroom picker stopping in at the dump at sundown could take home snapshots of five or six any day of the week, Fran never seemed to have been anywhere at just that right moment to actually see a bear.

Judson secretly wanted his wife to have her bear, though nothing like as desperately as she herself. But it would never do to let her know that, and he was goddamned if he was going to be suckered into getting his knickers in a knot about it. Nevertheless he retrieved the glasses from their bird-watching place on the kitchen counter and delivered them to the bedroom window, where Fran's tiny tramtrack figure was practically falling out of her nightdress in excitement.

"There, Judson, you look. I can't see through these things with my glasses on."

"Neither can I if you don't keep still and quit jumping up and down like a nun at a wedding," he flashed back irritably. "Now calm down and tell me where to look."

"Up there by the big tree," she said, stabbing at the window with her pointing finger. "I saw it move. Can you see it?"

"There's a hundred thousand trees up there, for Pete's

sake, and most of 'em are big. Start with the gully. Where do we go from there?"

"Half way up, about three inches to the left. No, the right. Can you see that bare patch shaped like a fry-pan?"

"If three inches means about two hundred yards, yes I can see it. And I guess your bear's that dark blob at the top?"

"That's it. I saw it move just before you came in. It's probably browsing."

Judson put down the glasses on the antique dressing table, carefully to avoid scratching the surface. "Well congratulations," he said with heavy irony. "This brings your score to seventy four rocks, not to mention two logging trucks and god knows how many stumps."

"Oh, you always make fun of me," she said petulantly, although she smiled a little. "Can't you let me see one just once?"

Judson whacked her rump playfully with the flat of his big hand. "Wish I could, Fran, but that hillside's getting on for half a mile away. Bears don't come that big. Why don't you set up camp at the dump? Stay a week or so, you're bound to see one. 'Less he sees you first. Either way you'll have a story to tell."

"Go away," Fran said. "I'm going to feed the birds. Get out of here while I put some clothes on."

Even if the bears refused to cooperate, Fran knew she could rely on the birds. All year round the garden was a drop-in centre for migrants. Most of them dropped in twice, on their way north and again south in the fall, and Fran kept a diary of arrival and departure dates and worried about them if they were a few days late. Friends from the city squeaked with delight at the humming birds, and sat impatiently by the feeders with cameras ready focused, and chatted noisily enough to deter all but the starving. But to Fran the highlight of the year was the arrival of the swallows, seldom a day late or early, a day filled with wheeling and diving and tentative visits to the nesting box above the greenhouse and much twittering and exclamations of delight that last year's home was still there and still untenanted.

The nesting box was built in an architectural style that Hillis Usry, who had a degree in Education and knew almost everything, designated Trad. Trad meant it was a miniature of the traditional suburban home, with plywood walls and sloping shingled roof, though Hillis evidently chose to overlook the tiny circular opening with its horizontal perch protruding below. Trad was in contrast to the greenhouse, which was Sawmill Gothic and made of the two-by-four scraps that were always available for the taking at the mill. The house, like the others that still survived near the tracks, was Railroad Renaissance, built mainly of lumber filched decades before from the CPR and resting on foundations of railroad ties.

For years Fran had been putting out food for the birds, wrestling with her conscience because attracting them only made it easier for Wolfgang Amadeus Meeowzart to catch his weekly quota. This fall she had borrowed hammer and nails and chicken wire from Judson's workshop and constructed Jackass Creek's most elegant free lunch counter in the giant Douglas fir at the south edge of the back yard. The Douglas fir stood just beside the fence, two twin trunks joined at a fork three feet above the ground. Across the fork Fran had nailed a plywood shelf and then festooned the trunk below with anti-cat chicken wire. Enough to snare a Sherman tank, Judson said.

It was there that Judson found her as he fumed up the garden path after making the discovery. "Be darned if the school kids haven't been after the apples again," he announced accusingly as if Fran had something to do with it. "Trampled down the fence and broke off the lower branches. That racoon face little thug from across the tracks, I bet, the one broke into the Baxter place. Or Joe Whatsisname from the reserve. What's his name? Joe something."

"You mean Jake Parker," Fran said. "There's no reason to suppose it's him, or anyone else from the reserve. You might as well blame the fruit pickers."

Every year there was an invasion from the city of anonymous predators in pick-up trucks who plundered the plum trees that were the last remaining vestiges of the gardens of Jackass Creek as it once had been. The fruit pickers plundered fast and left as soon as their trucks were full, and they usually took the blame for whatever no-one else would admit to. Even out of season.

"I'm going out and see if I can't track'm down, whoever they are," Judson said truculently. "Kids though, I bet."

Fran rearranged the chicken wire, mildly scolding Amadeus who had strolled over to inspect the arrangements.

A pair of Stellar's jays scolded in return from somewhere above her head. "You're such a grump, Judson. Didn't you ever go scrumping? Not once?"

"How come you always have to jump to everyone's defence? Somebody did it, and it sure as aitch wasn't me." Judson glowered at her. "You always want to see the best in everyone."

"Of course, Judson. I have to, living with you." Fran turned to him, looked at his scowling face and smiled. "Come on now, Judson. Didn't you?"

"What?"

"Go scrumping."

"Sure, me and Elmer Winston used to go scrumping after school, but there was empty lots even then, people moved away and left their gardens behind. And we never broke down no fences. Had more sense in those days. There was one time me and Elmer stayed out all night."

Fran sensed the onset of another monologue, and prepared to twist her ankle in the tangled undergrowth in self-defence. But launch was aborted at M minus one by a northbound freight approaching the crossing near the school, blasting its mandatory air-horn warning, "Dah-dah-de-dah," not blast-and-get-it-over-with, but long and drawn out and insolent and paralysing.

Like everyone else within earshot Judson gave up the attempt to talk. He turned and stumped off down the path to the gate at the end of the garden. Every year at about this time the gate began to stick in its frame and he had to kick it open. By the time the really cold weather arrived it would be stuck fast for the duration. As he did every year, Judson made a mental note to fix it in the spring. He turned into the back lane and walked between the ruts toward the unconverted school bus where Old Art Collins lived.

Art spent most of his day holding court beside the front wheel in a rocking chair some thoughtful soul had rescued from the dump. At ninety three he liked to call himself a retired professional man. He had been, in fact, a professional hermit. "Thought I'd move into Town for some company," he had explained. Twelve houses and a rusted out school bus would seem like Town after the solitude of Art's shack three miles out along the tracks. "Real nice little spot right here," was Art's considered opinion. "Gets too crowded the other side of the tracks."

There were thirty two houses and three trailers on the other side of the tracks. They were the village proper, where each owned the land it sat upon. Their owners were the Outsiders, the Johnny-come-latelies, few of whom went back further than a dozen years. The side where Art and Judson lived was owned entirely by the railway. Had been, as Tinfish Buckley learned to say when he flew in the Navy, since Pontius was a pilot. People owned their own houses; but as they moved away or died and stopped paying ground rent the Volunteer Fire Brigade moved in and burned down the houses for practice, and more priceless examples of Railroad Renaissance architecture were lost to posterity.

Judson stepped over Art's Saint Bernard, which lay like a second hand rug across the path, and sat on the step of the bus. "You got enough firewood to take you through,

Art?"

Art Collins considered. "Depends," he said. "Can't ever have too much. Speshully if it's ready cut." He looked at the wood pile, and back at Judson. "Ready cut's the important part. John Jack dropped off a load of logs last week. Nice fella, John. But I sure as hell don't need the exercise cutting it."

"I'll bring the splitter round later and we'll get it all cut up," Judson said. "You seen any kids around, after the apples? Bust my fence all to blazes."

"Ain't seed a kid round here in a month of Sundays. Kids are scared of me. Reason why I like it here. No kids, just dogs." Art grinned like a Halloween lantern, tried to spit tobacco juice through toothless gums and wiped a week-old chin with his sleeve. "Want to get yourself a good noisy dog. Wonderful for keeping the kids away. Want a beer?"

It was evening before Fran found the time to go outside again to her birds. The air had cooled suddenly as the sun dropped behind the mountains at the west wall of the valley. "Like the sun's just drowned hisself in the Almighty's slop bucket," as Joe Bundy once put it in a rare moment of lucidity unlaced with obscenity. Bundy was the mainstay of the beer parlour and his utterances, if they were noted at all, were remarkable more for their alcoholic incoherence than for literary colour.

With the sun hidden behind the ridge, the shadow of the mountain reached across the canyon and began to climb the steep face toward the highway. The sudden chill told Judson it was time to put away and wash up and change into clothes that Fran would allow on the living room chairs. As he approached the Douglas fir he found Fran there again, servicing her bird-table from the wicker basket she always used.

"Judson," she called without looking round, sensing his approach up the path. "Judson, they really cleaned me out today. I put out bird seed and grapes and nuts and bread crusts and everything's gone."

"Jays most likely," Judson said. "Squirrels too, maybe. Guess they know when they're onto a good thing. Sure playing you for a sucker." He went on into the house to wash under the tap in the kitchen sink.

"Don't wash your dirty hands all in among my clean dishes," Fran would scold whenever she caught him. But he had never been able to break the habit. His mother had always insisted, "Take off the dirt in the kitchen, then wash up pretty in the bathroom." That was the way it always had been, and that was the way it always seemed to be. Besides, the kind of dirt he got on his hands needed dishwashing detergent, not soap.

It was as he moved into the bathroom that he heard Fran call. There was no way he could understand her at that distance and he was certainly not about to go outside with dripping hands and arms. She called again, nearer. He dried his hands and went into the kitchen as she came in the door, breathless and excited, bursting with news.

"Judson, all these years you've laughed at me, and now you're going to have to eat crow."

"You've seen another bear," Judson mocked. "I can

tell by your face."

"I have, Judson, I have." She was ecstatic. "It's real this time."

"Let me guess," he said. "On the tracks. Climbing out of a caboose."

"You're an old fool," she said crossly, but her smile was like a spring crocus opening in the morning sun. "Quick, come and see. And don't make a noise."

He followed her outside, preparing more sarcasm but not so sure as he had been. Fran stopped at the fence by the Douglas fir. Her wicker basket lay under the tree where she had dropped it. "Want to go in and fetch my basket?" she challenged. "Look. Up there." She pointed up into the tree. The lowest branches were no more than twelve feet above the ground, fanning symmetrically like the spokes of a great umbrella. The form draped casually across two boughs was, undoubtedly, a bear, a yearling probably, deserted by its mother.

"Cheese!" Judson grabbed her and stepped back a pace. "That's too damn close to be comfortable. How long's he been there?"

"Do you know, I think he must have been there all day." Fran was bubbling over by now. "He must have come down to clean up the nuts and grapes and things and then gone back up. Now you know who stole the apples."

"And broke down the fence. Cheese, Fran, were you standing right underneath him?"

"He was right over my head," she said, shivering delightedly. "I was putting out more grapes and stuff and I heard a noise and I thought it must have been the jays and when I looked up he was staring me right in the eye. Oh Judson, isn't it exciting?"

"Altogether too damn exciting." Judson took her by the arm and moved her toward the house. "Do you know how quick a Bruin like that can shin down the tree and start making hamburger? Get up on the verandah and open the side door."

"What are you going to do, Judson? Don't do anything silly now."

"Don't worry about me." They were at the verandah steps. "I'm right with you. And if I didn't think you'd blab to everybody I'd be right up there ahead of you."

At that point Fran had to make one of the most difficult decisions of her life—whether to stay at the door and watch HER BEAR, or whether to rush to the telephone and start spreading the news. She compromised. "Don't you go away, Judson. You watch that bear and tell me everything he does."

"I'll tell you one thing he's going to do. He's going to get the hell out of here before the day's out. That's a dangerous animal, Fran, not a teddy bear."

"Judson," she wailed. "You can't chase him away. He's my First Bear. I want him to stay." For the remainder of the evening the McIntyre property resembled a tourist resort.

"You got a Disneyland franchise going here?" Harvey Kopichek yelled from the window of his pick-up as he drove onto the front lawn. Nine children, a baby, a pregnant wife and a German shepherd flowed out of the truck, and the dog headed yelping for the fence beneath the bear tree. Kopichek reached into the cab of the pick-up and brought out a hunting rifle and a box of shells. "Sure glad I wasn't working tonight. This'll make the fourth bear I bagged this week. Got three out at the dump the other day."

Judson stepped down from the verandah to meet him as he came into the back garden. "Harvey," he said quietly so that no-one else could hear, "you're welcome to come visiting, and the kids, even the dog so long as he don't chase the cat. But do me a favour and put that gun back in the truck."

Kopichek looked at him like a fox discovering chicken was off the menu. "You've got to be kidding, Jud. Won't be another chance like this for years, mebbe."

"Tough titty, Harvey." Judson turned him about and headed him toward the truck. "There's altogether too damn much killing round here. Four cats, two dogs, three bears, and one of your kids was heaving rocks at a kitten yesterday. Seems to me some of you people kill anything that moves."

Kopichek stopped at the pick-up. "What is it, Jud? You afraid of guns?"

"Sure am," Judson said grimly. "Just like I'm afraid of idiots who ain't afraid of guns. I'll tell you something else. One, nobody's bringing a gun onto my place. Two, nobody's banging one off anywhere around while I'm here. Three, that's Fran's bear and she don't want him killed. And you may as well have number four, get that damn yapping dog out of here before he scares the bear into doing something nasty."

Fran was already in bed reading when Judson finally came into the bedroom after locking up for the night. "I saw you sending Harvey away," she said. "Did he want to kill the bear?"

"Hard to fault him really," Judson said. "Bear's not the sort of thing they want around the village, with all the kids about. Even if they are breeding like a tribe of gophers. It'll have to go."

Fran began a sharp retort, then decided to change the subject. "You're late. What have you been doing?"

"Thought I'd strip the rest of the apples off the tree," he said. "Don't want Bruin tearing the tree apart. Don't want to waste the apples, either."

"Were there many left?"

"Enough."

"Enough for what?"

"Fill a basket."

"Where did you put it? You didn't leave it out, did you?"

Judson looked down at her, her eyes still shining after the second most wonderful day of her life. He turned away, wondering how best to tell her.

"Left them under the tree. Sort of a thanksgiving present. Thought maybe he'll stick around a little longer if we treat him right."

Fran's eyes filled with tears. "You're an irascible old devil," she said softly. "But you're a lovely man."

THE TOMATO PATCH

A long time back in Hillis Usry's youth, back when the greenhouse effect only interested gardeners and crepitating cows were pastoral pleasantries and not yet perambulating methane factories, back, in fact, when the world was more ignorant if not more innocent, Hillis became enthralled by a certain joke in a magazine.

"Paw," says the lady of the house. "there's a powerful bad smell. Must be the drains."

"Can't be the drains, Maw," says Paw. "This house ain't got no drains."

Hillis thought this sample of rural corn was the funniest thing to enter his life since Uncle Clayton flushed his false teeth down the toilet. The memory of it must still have been with him that halcyon August evening when Shawna announced with commendable calmness, "Hillis, the washing machine's backing up. The drains must be blocked."

"Can't be the drains, Honey," Hillis replied with instant glee. "This house ain't got no drains," and thereupon collapsed into the basket chair and laughed till he cried, and then saw the aggravation on Shawna's face and woke to the realisation that he had a problem indeed.

It was in a way fortunate that the house Hillis and Shawna had bought two years earlier from Old Man Jeffries had no utility room. When the house was first built it was not even the fashion to install a bathroom, or a kitchen for that matter. So the washing machine was boarding out on the verandah outside the kitchen door. And though the kitchen floor had long ago begun sloping to the north, the verandah had somehow subsided southward and the laundry water was cascading conveniently out into the yard.

Hillis Usry was principal of Jackass Creek Primary School, the cosy four room focus of all the village, community activity. To the locals of Jackass Creek, Hillis typified an educated man, with his rimless glasses and receding hairline and a fringe of beard round an insignificant chin. He had studied a great many things in his thirty four years, attended two universities and achieved two degrees. But of the elementary principles of plumbing he knew as much or as little as King Solomon knew about celibacy. He was not even sure whether there were indeed any drains, though he suspected they would be an unlikely luxury.

It was just when Hillis was standing forlornly in his back yard, wondering where water from the washing machine was supposed to go when it was not sloshing down the verandah steps, and whether a Master's degree in Education was sufficient qualification for running away and joining the Foreign Legion, that John Jack happened out onto the back porch of the house next door. It seemed that whenever Hillis had a problem, the big friendly Native just happened to be there.

"Having a spot of trouble, Hillis?" John would ask, his large mouth grinning shyly, and then he would stroll over and there would be no more problem. Hillis had only to be changing the wheel of the ancient Toyota and John would suddenly be standing there watching. "Having a spot of trouble, Hillis?" and somehow it would be Hillis standing there watching while John changed the wheel.

But the trouble with John Jack was that Hillis never seemed to be able to do anything for him in return. Neither he nor May would visit. Shawna had invited them in for coffee, for Thanksgiving, to parties, but they seemed to prefer to keep to themselves. And so, the more John helped out in a hundred ways, the less Hillis could bring himself to ask another favour.

So when Hillis Usry saw the stocky figure in the MacDonalds tee-shirt and Budweiser cap he was both relieved and embarrassed, because he was certainly having a spot of trouble at that moment. But at that moment there was no large grin on John Jack's walnut face.

"Those cows been into your place last night, Hillis?" he called.

"Not that I know of," Hillis said. "Haven't really looked yet. They been around again?"

"Whole herd must've been in. Ate all my beans and trampled everything else."

A helicopter throbbed suddenly overhead, low enough to kill conversation. Hillis walked across to the next yard and joined his neighbour on the porch.

"Damn helicopters!" John yelled. "Like flies around a moose turd, the way they flock around here."

The Fraser Canyon, with its flanking mountains rising three thousand feet each side of the village of Jackass Creek, provided a natural flight way for aircraft of all kinds. But it was usually the helicopters that flew so low, sometimes below treetop height, climbing steeply to vault the invisible power lines across the river decked out with their spherical orange markers. Tinfish Buckley, who owned the hotel across the river in Stretton and was an authority on everything that flew except birds, called the canyon 'Whirlybird Alley.' Tinfish had got his nickname flying in the Navy, where he misspent part of his youth dropping torpedoes and dreaming of owning a pub.

"Even the Air Force couldn't get lost along here with two railroads and a river to follow," he would tell patrons of the pub with the Voice of Experience. And the patrons would nod and agree that it was so.

"What are we going to do about those cows, Hillis?" John Jack demanded when the noise level had diminished to a steady grumble from the diesel locomotives that seemed to roost for hours and even days on the railroad tracks that shared the canyon with the river and the highway. "They're eating up everyone's garden, and Phillips won't keep them penned up. He's got a damn great bull with them now, and he's mean."

"Phillips or the bull?"

"Both. Phillips really gets pleasure out of screwing people. He's screwed so many people they named the Phillips screwdriver after him. You know I counted twenty three cows in your school yard yesterday, and that's a lot of cow pats for the kids to step in."

"When they get spooked by a dog that's a lot of beef to have stampeding through the village," Hillis said. "The children are liable to get hurt." To Hillis his charges were always 'children.' He could never bring himself to call them 'kids.'

The Great Jackass Creek Cattle War had already been playing for several months. It was a drama of the greed and arrogance of the landowning class against the righteous impotence of the working peasantry according to Harvey Kopichek, who had a large wife and family and lived right beside the school. Harvey had already been to see the RCMP Corporal over in Stretton on the other side of the river.

It was the Head Horseman's reading of the situation that Jackass Creek was open range country and Willard Phillips was within his legal if not his moral rights. And Phillips evidently knew his rights where his cows were concerned, and was prepared to milk them to the last quart.

"We've got to do something about that arrogant bastard," John Jack vowed that blue August evening as the sun prepared to drop into the great pit that must lie behind the mountain skyline before the evening chill swept across the valley. "He's in the beer parlour every night, what say we steam over and pin his ears back?"

Hillis shuffled from one foot to the other and then back again, a certain sign of Usry embarrassment. "Would you mind if we put it off till tomorrow?" he suggested diffidently. "My washing machine's backing up." Instantly the dark brown scowl rearranged itself into the familiar grin. "Well let's get at it, Hillis," John said cheerfully. "Sounds like the septic tank. Where is it?"

But of course Hillis had no foggiest idea where the septic tank might be, or even whether he really was the owner of a septic tank. Nothing had so far overflowed or collapsed or produced identifiable odours. Until that day it had apparently behaved with exemplary efficiency, unlike much of the rest of the Usry establishment. Within a month of buying his house from Old Man Jeffries, who had quickly moved to another province, Hillis had nailed a handsome hand-carved name plate to a post in the front yard.

"Faulty Towers," it said. The Usrys claimed the only house in Jackass Creek with its own name and at least two major faults requiring attention at any one time. As his lease made clear, at least to a schoolteacher who knew his decimals, the house sat on one point seven five of an acre of land. And the septic tank, if there was one, could be anywhere inside that boundary. Or even outside.

"Even under the house, the way things are around here," as Hillis said. "Or it could all be pouring into a hole in the ground. This house is a monstrosity wrapped up in an enigma." Winston Churchill had expressed a similar sentiment, but as far as Hillis Usry was concerned Churchill was a Grade 'A' plagiarist.

They began by exploring the yard for signs of excessive growth where a septic tank might have overflowed, but all too soon the sun was well down behind the mountain rim and the twilight had that thinness of imminent expiry.

"Let's quit and get down to it first thing tomorrow," John Jack suggested. "My shift doesn't start till four. Can Shawna wait till then for the laundry?"

Hillis owed much of his make-up to an ancestry of puritanical farmers who thrived on a diet of guilt and mental self-flagellation. But the upwelling blush of guilt at the prospect of pre-empting John's limited leisure time was cut off at the source by the chilling news that shrilled from the bathroom window at that moment.

"Hillis, come quick, the toilet's backing up!"

Once again it was John Jack who came to the rescue, and added to the mounting guilt. "May'll get the guest room ready," he pronounced. "Move in with us. Can't have Shawna peeing her pants. We'll fix it in the morning."

May was bottling early plums, so Shawna went into the kitchen to help.

"You think we should go talk to Phillips?" John asked when the two men found they were left to keep the cat company. And Hillis began another guilt attack at the realisation that he had not even kept John's problem on the back burner while John had been helping with his.

Across the bridge in Stretton, the Pub was cool and dim. Tinfish Buckley had learned in the Navy not to expect a man to do anything he would not do himself, so by eight every evening he was at his own special table, and occasional tipplers, in search of convivial company, were always welcome to join the group which gathered round him. The drifters and spongers, who were less particular about the company they kept, tended to sit at the bar with Willard Phillips and drink their fill in sycophantic symbiosis.

When John Jack and Hillis Usry arrived they were naturally drawn to where Tinfish sat in serious discussion with Justin McIntyre and Culwinder Parmar. There were few subjects more serious or worthy of discussion that summer than the privatization of highways maintenance by the Provincial Government. Tinfish supported the government. The pub patrons in general agreed that although Tinfish was an exceptionally likable fellow, good hearted, generous, great company, there must be something fundamentally disturbed about a man who agreed with everything the government did. And Tinfish not only agreed, he voted for them and even gave them extra money in addition to what they extorted in income tax.

"We were talking about the money this government wastes," Cully explained when they had agreed it was a cool one but still the right kind of night for drinking beer. "Tinfish doesn't seem to mind pouring his profits down a big hole in the ground."

"I haven't noticed Hillis complaining when they pour money into the schools," Tinfish said.

"They don't pour it into the schools," Hillis objected. "They trickle it in."

"They pour a damn sight too much into day-care, I'll tell you that much," said Judson. "Day-care's doing more to harm this country than all the drugs and crime and pollution put together."

"This sounds like the start of one of your monologues," John said, filling his glass from the jug beside Hillis.

"How long's it going to take? We've got to see a man about a cow."

"You can leave any time you want." Judson stared back truculently from beneath brows that should have been pruned back the season before. "Day-care just encourages both parents to go out to work, right? So the older kids come home from school and there's no-one home. It ain't home unless there's someone to come home to. So the kids go back out. You know why kids get into trouble with drugs? Because their parents don't give a damn. How many parents know where their kids are, what they're doing? When I was a kid my parents played games with us round the kitchen table. Cards, board games, word games. And we talked. Now when they come home from work they don't want to do nothing but sit with their mouths hanging open in front of the box. No conversation, no teaching about morals or behaviour or doing the right thing. Leave that for teachers to do. But that's not the worst of it. What about the little kids at day-care? Spend most of their waking day with strangers. There's kids around this town get farmed out every day when they should be still on the tit. Don't even know which is their mother. And they wonder why we've got so many disturbed kids. And juvenile crime."

"You going to stop for a breather now, Judson?" Cul-winder Parmar was a Sikh. He never argued. He preferred to ask questions. "What should we do about it?"

"Stop both parents going out to work." Judson drained his glass. Tinfish filled it from the jug and signalled for a refill. "I don't care which one works, but pay one of them to stay home with the kids. Someone should be bringing up the kids better than they are. Reduce the unemployment, save money on welfare, reestablish family life, improve kids' behaviour, reduce crime …."

"But isn't that infringing on human rights?" John Jack liked to needle Judson.

"Piss on human rights. What about the rights of a little kid to grow up in a decent family situation? And you forgot to ask me what about the poor people on the poverty line who need both parents working to afford the television and the VCR and the dishwasher and the second car. What's wrong with everyone taking a cut in their standard of living?"

There is no knowing what depths of heresy might have been plumbed if the arrival of Joe Bundy had not disrupted the meeting. Bundy, who lived in a decaying school bus in Jackass Creek, had managed to carve out a successful career of living off welfare. And off everyone else. Tinfish suddenly decided he had to do some work in the office. Cully and Judson said they were just leaving anyway. And John and Hillis fortunately remembered why they were there in the first place. Bundy found himself alone at the table, and since buying his own beer seemed like an unrewarding way of spending the evening he moved on to brighten the lives of a group of loggers from up-river.

"You talk to Phillips," John said. "Me and him don't talk the same language. He doesn't like Natives for a start."

"Where will you be?" Hillis asked.

"I'll be in the Willard."

"The what?"

"The Willard. I don't believe in calling it the John," said John. "See what you can do."

Hillis decided it might be politic to arrive bearing

gifts. He bought two glasses of suds and walked across to where Phillips sat, a six foot beer belly on a five foot eight frame, a neck that started above the chin and a complexion like a western sunset.

"Evening, Willard," he said, concealing the effort it cost him to use the man's first name. "Drink?"

"What's this for?" Phillips demanded.

Hillis shuffled from one foot to the other and back again. "I wondered if we could talk about a problem we have in the village," he said, instantly certain this was not going to be the right opening.

"Your problem or mine?"

"Sort of everyone's, really," Hillis said. "We're wondering if we can come to some sort of friendly arrangement about your cattle before any of the children get hurt."

"Tell the kids to keep out of the way, it's that easy." Phillips looked as friendly as a pit bull with tooth-ache, and a friendly arrangement seemed unlikely. "This is open range country. It's up to you to fence your yard if you don't like cattle."

"I was thinking more of the school," Hillis said mildly.

"So fence the bloody school."

"Couldn't we maybe work something out?" Hillis persevered. "It's such a pity to have bad feeling in the village."

"Your problem not mine." Phillips turned away. "Work something out if you've a mind to, but leave me out of it."

Hillis bit back a reply. There was no point in pleading further. He turned away, feeling defeated and disgusted with himself for being so ineffectual. He wanted to hit the man, knock him off his stool. Phillips deliberately ignored him and reached for the full glass that was to have been a peace offering.

"I'll take that," Hillis said quickly, and grabbed the glass. "It's too good for a clod like you." With deliberate calm he carried it to where Joe Bundy sat. "Compliments of Mr. Phillips," he said loudly, and stalked across to join John Jack at the door.

Hillis slept fitfully in John Jack's guest room. It could have been the beer, or the strange bed, or the cows. But there were cows galloping across his classroom and herding the children into a corner when John's voice broke into his dreams next morning. It was some moments before he could remember where he was. He had never been in the Jacks' guest room before, and waking in a strange bed was not a pastime he had been accustomed to in his youth. John was hammering on his door.

"We've struck pay dirt," John was calling. "Get up, I'll show you where the septic tank is."

"How embarrassing," Shawna said. "He's been digging up the garden while we were still asleep. Do hurry."

The big india rubber grin had expanded even further when it greeted Hillis outside the bedroom door. "Hillis, I think we just might have solved ourselves a few problems."

"You've found the septic tank already?" Hillis was still foggy with sleep. "Have you been up all night?"

But John was too full of good news to waste time answering questions. "You know that tomato patch at the bottom of your yard? Well forget it. You won't be getting tomatoes this year. Right where your tomatoes used to be is a nasty wet hole with a very unhappy cow up to her armpits in the finest manure."

Hillis Usry was not normally given to the baser emotions. But as he gazed at the exhausted cow and the wreckage of his septic tank that early morning his whole being became bathed in a glow of exultation. Overcoming the urge to shout with glee he turned to his neighbour and said very quietly, "John, I think we're going to screw that bastard Phillips right where it hurts."

Within three minutes he was back in the house and dialling Willard Phillips' number.

"Phillips? Hillis Usry. Did I get you out of bed? ... Oh, sorry you feel like that about it. I thought you might like to know one of your cows is in trouble. Drowning in my septic tank .... Which one? I've only got one septic tank ... Oh, which cow. Don't know really. Sort of manure coloured, that sound like one of yours? ... Better get round here quickly, she's not looking too good ...West end of my garden ...You'll be able to reach over the fence from the back lane and hoist her out with a crane ... No, sorry old chap, not having a crane inside my garden. Or a truck. It's all under cultivation ... Abso-bloody-lutely not, old chap, you try and set foot in my garden and I'll have you for trespass ... I'm sure I don't know where you're going to get hold of a crane, I'm just a schoolteacher, not a logger ... I don't think the phone company would be very happy about language like that, Mr. Phillips. Oh, by the way, you'll need someone to empty out the septic tank so you can get at the cow. Mr. Jack says he'll be happy to do it for you, he's very reasonable, a couple of hundred should cover it. And you'll need someone to put a sling round the cow so you can hoist her ... Certainly not, no way are any of your people coming into my garden, Mr. Phillips. But Mr. Jack says he'll be happy to help out in any way he can, say another two hundred? ... You could be right, Mr. Phillips, there's a lot of screwing going on these days. And by the way, Mr. Jack says he'd like cash in advance, if it's all the same to you, just in case. Can't be too careful, you know. See you in a little while, then. Oh, Mr. Phillips, you have a nice day, you hear?"

It was two days later that Hillis answered the phone and found himself talking to Harvey Kopichek. "Thought you might like to know there's an epidemic of septic tank disease in the village," Harvey said. "We're all having to open them up and leave the tops off for a few days. Very dangerous for cows. I'll let Phillips know, just in case he wants to keep his at home."

WEEDS

The rain in Spain, it seemed, had moved to Jackass Creek.
It had been raining continuously for three weeks, so Judson
McIntyre had been forced to do household chores for Fran
instead of pottering in his beloved garden. But finally the
weather had broken, and the garden was once more a place
for consuming cold ones.

Judson stepped out of the house feeling like a trog-
lodyte coming out into the sunlight, and looked over at the
ragged mass of closely growing greenery that was separating
his garden from the Disaster Site. It was already four feet
high, lush with it's unaccustomed watering.

"Artichokes, only put them in two years ago," Judson
confided over a cold one to Hillis Usry. "John Jack said they're
good to eat, and I always liked the idea of dollars and cents
growing in the garden. Tried to eat them last year, but no
way! Some things I just can't stomach, and artichokes is one.
Fran likes them. But then Fran likes dandelion leaves. And
garlic and stinky cheese. And chitlings, and oolichans and
sheep's brains and haggis and ...."

"I thought they were Sunflowers when I saw them
blooming last year," Hillis interrupted hurriedly to avoid further details of Fran's indiscretions. "Great big yellow flowers.
They must be hardy to survive these winters."

"Hardy? I'll say! And they spread like flies on a cow
pat." In fact, the artichokes had spread far enough to form a

four foot high hedge between Judson McIntyre and the Disaster Site. But it would be a few years before the hedge would be tall enough to mask completely the view of rusting car bodies and emasculated motors and tangled logging cables and empty beer cases that had decorated Tom Brannigan's back yard ever since he moved in three years earlier.

The Disaster Site was a burden on the soul of Judson McIntyre that hot July afternoon, and every afternoon, a continuing burden that nevertheless was unable to reduce his thirst. He went into the house and brought out two more cold ones. Judson had tried reasoning with his neighbour. But Brannigan was seldom in a condition to understand reasoning. Judson had tried threatening legal action. But Brannigan had threatened dire retaliation of a more physical kind, against Judson, against Fran, and against Fran's beloved cats.

Judson McIntyre had been a fireman on the CPR before he was promoted to engineer. He was a big man, with long arms and a no-nonsense manner. But Tom Brannigan was a logger, with red eyes and well used fists and a violent temper, and he kept a hunting rifle just inside the front door of his house.

Judson was in bed by ten o'clock and up at six every morning, and lived for his wife and his garden. Brannigan was in his own bed as seldom as he could arrange it, and lived for other people's wives and attracted junk the way Old Art Collins's dog attracted fleas. His behaviour was unpredictable when he was drinking, which was six times a week and twice on Sundays, so Judson McIntyre, though hating himself for giving in to intimidation, was not about to initiate any sort of confrontation.

"Talked to the Head Horseman," Judson told Hillis. "But the Corporal says it ain't against the law to keep junk in your yard. Sure as shootin' he's selling drugs, there's so many trucks come calling. The Corporal says to take their numbers, but you know these yokels on this side of the river never bother to buy a licence. Just wish there was something I could pin on him."

The RCMP were in Stretton, across the river where the highway went through on the east side of the canyon. Stretton boasted a hotel and a store and a gas station and a post office. And a high school that sprawled under the fall-out from the burner at the sawmill. And a stretch of highway that was guaranteed to net a dozen speeding tickets any time there was a police car to spare. So the three Mounties were kept busy enough without crossing the river to check on a hundred and fifty people in the village of Jackass Creek where the post office and the hotel and the station had long since closed.

It was after Judson had been away for five days visiting Fran's sister in Kamloops that his concern with the artichokes and the Disaster Site was transferred to something else. The something else was The Weeds. They were an embryo forest, sprouting between the stems of the artichokes. They were all the more noticeable because they must have been the only weeds in Judson's garden. Weeds were not allowed in Judson's garden. If any dared to venture across the boundary they were promptly grabbed by the throat and evicted, so Judson was rightly affronted by this invasion from

110

outer space.

"Spray the whole lot with weed killer," Hillis suggested. "It'll kill the artichokes as well, but you don't want to eat them anyway."

"Can't use weed killer," Judson said firmly. "Fran won't have me use weed killer." Judson was a big man, five foot eleven inches tall, with an aggressive chin and a personality to match. Fran was a slight, almost frail looking figure in her home made cotton dresses, peering sternly over the top of wire rim glasses with her head down and her eyebrows raised. But ever since the second year of their marriage, forty six years earlier, Judson had deferred to his wife in all things.

"If Fran don't want it, that's all there is to it," he would say. "I don't argue with her. Don't even make decisions any more. Used to try, but they were always wrong. Leave decisions to Fran, saves a lot of argument. I remember one time, we hadn't been married more'n a few months. Just moved into this house Fran was complaining about how the kitchen cupboards were always designed by men. She was so short she couldn't reach the shelves. Remember the song? 'Five foot two, eyes of blue.' I used to sing it to her. Only she was five foot three, eyes of green. She went away for ten days to see her mother, so while she was away I took the kitchen cupboards apart and lowered them all, right down so's they sat on the counter. She didn't need the counter, there was that big kitchen table, it's still there. Well, you know what? She took one look and burst into tears. When she'd done, she tore me into strips because I'd taken away her counter space.

Never made a decision since, not where she's concerned. So if Fran don't like weed killer, got to find some other way of getting rid of them."

"Why not dig them up?" Hillis ventured, aware there must be a good reason why not.

"Take me a week, they're so mixed up with the artichokes, and the artichoke roots go so deep, that's why," Judson said truculently. "Guess that's what it'll have to be, though, or the weeds'll be all over the garden. Pity to lose the hedge, though." However, within a few days even The Weeds were relegated to secondary importance.

A fresh problem was developing. Hillis Usry and John Jack had brought round a case of cold ones, because it was one of the canyon's typical hot evenings. Hillis had not even sat down in the old home-made wooden garden chair before he began to shuffle bashfully from one foot to the other, a sure sign of Usry reluctance to speak his mind. But the Indian with the big friendly grin came straight to the point.

"Can't sit out here tonight, Judson, your yard stinks worse than a herd of skunks having a farting contest."

"Guess I've got used to it some," Judson said. "Better go inside. The steelhead are running and Brannigan's had an illegal net out. What he can't sell he dumps out in his yard with the rest of the junk. That bastard's becoming a real pain in the butt. Nothing quite as bad as stinking fish."

"Except a herd of skunks," John Jack insisted.

"Speaking as a teacher," Hillis said, "I must insist that skunks don't run in herds."

John Jack opened his can and took a long pull. "Speaking as a genooine Native First Nations Aboriginal Indian, and a long time tee-totaller to boot, I must insist that you're not educated till you've seen a herd of skunks stampeding across the prairie. My ancestors used to hunt them on horseback."

Hillis Usry and John Jack were neighbours in the road that ran beside the railway tracks. In the intervals when the growling diesels squatting on the siding moved north and left the canyon echoing with silence, they would argue until one or other gave in and fetched a cold one. They went up onto the verandah and into the house, where Fran was busy at the counter making biscuits.

Hillis took one last shot. "Are you quite sure you're not thinking of buffalo?"

Fran looked round. "What's he talking about?"

"He's trying to deny my heritage," John said.

It was two days later that the stinking fish in their turn moved to the back burner. Fran McIntyre's fridge stopped working.

"I've been putting away some money for a new cookstove," Fran said tearfully. "Now I guess it'll have to go to replace the fridge."

But Judson was enough of a handyman to check the fridge on another circuit. "Not the fridge," he pronounced. "It's the electric, must be the breaker." He climbed down the ancient steep steps to the Dungeon, a hole in the ground with a dirt floor and walls made of river boulders that housed the wood furnace and the water heater and the breaker box and a thousand spider webs. One of the circuit breakers had indeed been tripped. Judson reset it, and it tripped again. Judson looked at the cables leading into the breaker box, and swore under his breath. Fran refused to allow swearing, but not even Fran could control a man's thoughts.

One of the cables had been neatly stripped of insulation for two or three inches on either side of a blackened area. "Doggoned rat eating the insulation!" Judson declared. "Hope he electrocuted hisself." But there was no executed rodent anywhere to be seen. "Doggoned critter gets away with it once, he learns how to do it again and again," Judson grumbled.

Later that evening, John Jack heaved an empty can over the hedge into the Disaster Site, and carefully selected a full one from the cooler. "Probably expect a whole herd of rats now. Probably smelling the fish, and stampeding in from all over Jackass Creek to get at the free lunch."

Hillis Usry was more concerned with practical things. "Did you find out where he got into your cellar? Have to block up anywhere they can get in, or you'll be infested with them. Wire wool's the best thing, they don't like eating through that."

It was two days before Judson could get a bale of wire wool sent up from Barford, and the three of them set about rat-proofing the cellar. And then it was time for Judson to reluctantly shut up the house and accompany Fran on the annual visit to Fran's family in Manitoba. He hated to leave the garden for so long, but Hillis arranged to drop by to turn on the sprinklers and even mow the grass a couple of times.

To Judson, even a short time away from his garden seemed like as long as Fran's first pregnancy when she was puking five times a day for three months straight.

After ten days away, as Judson drove up the highway he occupied the time by picturing what the roses would look like and hoping Hillis had remembered his instructions not to get water on the leaves.

In Jackass Creek the big diesels still squatted on the tracks a quarter mile from the house, making the windows vibrate with their throbbing grumble. The roses certainly needed cutting back, and the Scarlet Runners were running out of control. But the feature that caught Judson's attention first, the moment he stepped out onto the back porch, was the artichoke hedge. The small forest of weeds that had been sprouting between the artichoke stems had miraculously become a large forest as high as the hedge itself. On closer inspection, they were like no weeds Judson had ever seen before. He and Fran were still examining them when Hillis Usry walked into the garden.

"Don't look like weeds at all, Hillis," Judson said as he opened a cold one. "What do you think they are?"

Hillis Usry laughed till he spilled his beer. "Quite a healthy crop," he said, and pulled off one of the leaves.

"But what the hell are they?" Judson demanded testily.

"Marijuana!" Hillis looked at Judson's face and spilled his beer again. "I don't suppose you planted them, so it looks like your friendly neighbourhood junk collector's started a new business."

"But that's illegal, ain't it?" The dawn of hope was in Judson's eyes.

"Certainly is."

"That's all I need, then. Something the Mounties can pin on him at last. I've got the bastard where I want him."

Hillis shook his head slowly. "I'm not so sure. I think maybe he's got you. Whose land is the hedge on?"

"Mine. He's trespassing. I can get him fer that, too."

"You can't prove he was trespassing. You can't prove he planted it. You can't prove it's his marijuana."

"But it's obviously his. Who else would have put it there?" Judson was indignant.

"How about you?"

"Eh?"

"It's on your land. It's in your hedge. He'll swear it's not his. He could even say he's seen you watering it."

Judson was appalled. "You mean he can grow his dope in my garden and I can't stick him with it?"

"He's got more chance of sticking you with it."

"But the Mounties know me. And they know him— he's got a record."

"Sorry Jud, you need proof. Maybe you'd better wait and catch him harvesting it."

Judson seethed with fury all that evening. "Growing it in my hedge!" he fumed at Fran, as if it was her fault. "I can't get him and he knows it. He's laughing at me right now, I shouldn't wonder."

Fran's head hardly came up to Judson's chest. With her small mouth and oversize spectacles she always reminded him of a diminutive owl. And her voice was diminutive to match.

"Sounds like her boiler pressure's down a few pounds," Judson would say.

But Fran's quiet reason often served as a steadying influence on Judson's impetuousness. She had already seen further into the problem as he stomped round the kitchen, thumping the counter with his fist in frustration.

"I think it might be even worse than that, dear," she said thoughtfully.

"What d'you mean?"

"If you confront him about this, or if you complain to him about his junk, or even if he takes offence about anything at all, and you know how touchy he is, he can go to the police and tell them there's marijuana in our garden."

"The Mounties wouldn't believe him."

"They'd be bound to investigate it, anyway. And you know what the village thought about those people across the tracks last year when the Mounties checked on them, and it turned out it wasn't even marijuana. You know how people talk, and how unpleasant some of them can be."

"Well, what if I go to the Mounties first and tell them I've only just found it?"

"I expect they'd believe you, dear. But Tom would never forgive us and he's already threatened to shoot the cats. It would be the same if you cut it all down or pulled it all out by the roots. He'd know it was you."

"Wouldn't put it past him to torch the house," Judson said bitterly.

"I think I'd almost rather that than have the cats hurt," Fran said, her eyes filling with tears at the thought. "Can't you just forget about it?"

"It's the principle of the thing, Fran. And what about when it's fully grown? He'll dry it, or whatever you do with the stuff, and start selling it around the village. Hillis won't want the school kids getting hold of it."

"Neither would we, dear," Fran said.

"Alright, there you are then. We've got to do something."

But before they could do something, anything, the Weeds in their turn were replaced as number one problem by what John Jack immediately designated The Eleventh Plague. The Plague manifested itself as a score of very groggy rats that were eating their way through the marijuana hedge and then heading for a second course in Fran's vegetable garden.

John Jack's brown face split in a broad grin when he saw them. "They've got the munchies," he said. "Marijuana does that to the appetite. Best dispose of them before they eat up all of Fran's garden. I don't think they'll be running very fast, more likely to be taking a nap on the lawn."

"Got a few choices, then," Judson said. "They're so dozy we can shoot 'em, trap 'em, whack 'em, throw 'em in the river, anything. We'll get old Art Collins's dog over. He hasn't caught anything faster than a turtle with arthritis in years. He'll think he's in heaven."

John shook his head. "That still leaves Brannigan. You don't want him to think it's you ruined his plants. You

118

want him to know it was the rats. If he knows his little relations are eating up his pocket money, even Brannigan's got enough sense to realise it's the fish that's attracting them. So he'll get rid of the fish. Then you'll get rid of the smell. And the rats. The rats have already mined the weeds. And that leaves the hedge to go on growing till it hides Brannigan's junk. Right?"

Judson was doubtful. "How's he going to know it was the rats?"

"Simple. We toss them over into the Disaster Site, right by Brannigan's back door. When he comes out this evening and finds a herd of hopped up rodents lying belly up on the doorstep, he'll know. He's stoopid, but he's not that stoopid."

KILLER

Joe Bundy's dog Killer was really at the center of it all. Killer, like Bundy himself, was usually high on the menu of topics to be hashed over as the faithful left the Jackass Creek village hall after the Thursday Bible meeting. The trouble with Bundy was alcohol, they all agreed. And the trouble with Killer was Bundy, who had a disposition like sandpaper and a grudge against all humanity that evidently infected his dog.

Bundy was a short, grouchy man with a red veined face, a bulbous red nose, watery red eyes and a neck as scrawny and red as a tom turkey's. Occasionally when he was sober his body leaned forward and his feet fell one in front of the other when he walked as if his legs were run by clockwork. More usually he lurched along from one tack to the other like a rudderless boat, muttering earnestly to himself and nodding his head as if he understood.

Killer was quite different. Killer was big and muscular, with a flattened face and a thick neck, and he never muttered. When he spoke it was with authority, his short front legs springing into the air with every bark so that he stomped the ground and the dirt flew to punctuate every word. He had never actually attacked anyone, but the villagers tended to judge by appearances and condemned him accordingly.

The two, Joe Bundy and Killer, lived in symbiotic isolation in a slightly converted school bus a few hundred yards from The Green House On The Hill. The Hill was really little more than a low knoll rising out of the glacial plateau half way down the canyon, and Judson McIntyre had painted the Green House pale blue at least five summers before. But it had been The Green House On The Hill since Judson and Fran moved in forty six years before and no-one in Jackass Creek was about to change the name. Besides, it was a better address than a five digit number on a street that no longer existed.

Jackass Creek was known to the County planners as a community in decline. In its heyday, with the houses of the railway officials on both sides of the tracks, and a hotel for passengers and a bunkhouse for train crews and a roundhouse and a maintenance yard, there had been plenty of work. But once the passenger trains stopped running and the roundhouse closed down the village began to die. The empty houses were mostly too old to live by themselves, so the volunteer fire department burned them down and the weeds and the wildflowers moved in and covered the ashes.

In the Green House On The Hill Fran McIntyre was preparing breakfast when Judson, dressed in his old denims and railway cap, came in from the garden holding a bunch of earthy carrots in his big hand. "Carrot fly getting at the carrots worse than ever this year," he announced as if it was Fran's fault. He dropped the carrots onto the counter by the sink and took off his cap. "Greenfly on the roses and leaf-rollers eating up everything else. Ever since you stopped me spraying it's been getting worse. Bugs are taking over the garden, Fran."

Fran had to look up at his face, his shaggy grey brows and long, aggressive chin were so far above her own. He seldom showed her a smile, but he was a gentle man and she loved him dearly.

"Come and get washed up, Judson. Biscuits'll be ready as soon as you are. I heard another rifle shot just now. Was that Joe Bundy, d'you think?"

"Sure to be," Judson said as he washed up at the kitchen tap. "Probably only shooting at crows again, but when he's drinking he gets mad at anything that moves. Hunting rifle's a dangerous thing at any time, but Bundy's a menace. He was down at the mail box yesterday, couldn't hardly stand up."

"I'm making plenty of biscuits so there'll be some for you to take round to him after breakfast." Fran believed most problems could be solved by a nourishing diet. "He's getting his carbohydrates from all that whisky, but he needs more vitamins. Did he eat all the apple pie you took round Saturday?"

"How should I know, Fran, I haven't been round there since. It ain't as if he was the kind of fella you drop in for a chat. I don't trust that dog of his either. Won't let anyone get near unless Bundy calls him off. Real vicious animal."

"Maybe it's being all alone with Joe that makes it like that? People aren't friendly to Joe, and dogs are sensitive to people's feelings. They can't help it."

"Fran, those darned rose colored glasses of yours make you blind sometimes. You don't even see anything wrong with Bundy, do you?"

"Well he's drinking too much, certainly. But that's probably because he's lonely." During forty six years of marriage to a man as irascible and intolerant as Judson, Fran

McIntyre had learned to see the best in everyone and make the best of every situation. She believed there was always something good to be found if you looked for it. If you wanted to find it.

While they were eating breakfast in the large kitchen with the old wood-burning range that Judson kept promising to haul away they heard more shots. The sound echoed from the canyon wall on the far side of the river where the highway clung to the sheer limestone face. In the crisp morning air, the explosive bark of the engine brakes of long distance trucks winding down the hill came clearly through the open window, but the sound of the shots was distinctive.

"Someone ought to take that gun away from the old fool," Judson said. "I'm not taking biscuits round there while he's in this mood. He's just as likely to take a pot shot at me or set the dog on me. Have to wait till he's emptied the bottle. Best put the biscuits in the freezer."

Fran wondered whether she had the courage to take them round herself. Joe would probably react differently to her. The dog, too. On the other hand they might not. Judson looked across at the slight tram-track figure in the bright red house coat he had bought her for Christmas, the greying hair and the owl-size glasses that magnified the green of her eyes, and permitted himself a thin smile. He could guess what she was thinking about. Worrying about Joe Bundy. Her life had always centred round doing things for other people. She had only retired from teaching two years before, when he retired from the railway, and he could sense how much she missed the children. Most days she would be back in Jackass Creek

Primary School supervising at lunchtime or taking cookies in for the teachers' recess snack.

"There's Joe's dog now, isn't it?" Fran exclaimed suddenly, pointing out of the window. "That black one? I wish Joe wouldn't let it run loose."

Judson jumped up from the table and ran out into the front yard, snatching up a saucepan from the counter as he passed. He had done this often enough, banging the pan with his fist and roaring till his throat hurt. The dog drew back its lips and snarled deep in its throat, then turned casually away and strutted off.

"Darned if I don't think he comes here just to make me mad," Judson muttered to himself. "Never misses a day."

The morning sun just showed over the top of the canyon and the edge of the mountain shadow was already clear of the yard, racing across the field toward the river a hundred yards away. The mist still hovered over the river and would stay there till the sun burned it off. Till then, too, the dew would remain on the ground, the birds would be quiet, the air would stay crisp and fresh, and the smoke from the burner at the sawmill across the river would plume purposefully up and away into the cooler air instead of flopping back down to blanket the valley in the dull blue fog of corporate profit.

It was later that evening, when Judson was in the back yard wishing someone would breed a variety of grass that stayed short for ever, that Fran's voice came faintly from inside the house. He had never known her to raise her voice, not even when the throbbing of the giant diesels squatting on the nearby tracks made the whole house vibrate with their noise, not even when the electricity failed in the middle of their favourite television program and they had to light the oil lamp. "That's why I married Fran," he would say. "She never gets steamed up enough to fog her glasses."

Judson growled and dropped the rake and went to the back door. "Give it to me again, Fran, and turn up the volume. I can't hear you outside."

"Kitty hasn't been in for his food. I haven't seen him all day. Have you seen him?"

"Can't say I have. Usually comes in by this time, don't he?"

"He never misses. I do hope he hasn't been run over or something."

"He's a survivor, that cat. Don't worry, he'll be back."

But the cat Fran loved like one of her children was not back by nightfall. The next morning Fran was in tears. "He's never stayed away as long as this. Go and see if you can find him, Judson, please. He may be lying hurt somewhere."

"Jeez, Fran, there's a lot of empty space round here. He could be anywhere."

"I'll come with you. No, I'll look by the river. You go and ask if anyone's seen him. And you can take those biscuits round to Joe Bundy at the same time."

There were less than a hundred and fifty people living in the whole of Jackass Creek, with the railroad dividing the village in two. On the east side of the tracks near the river only twelve houses fit to be occupied still survived, in addition to Joe Bundy's school bus. Judson canvassed the houses and searched the empty spaces where houses had stood in better days, hoping to find nothing that would break Fran's heart. At last he came to the place he had left till last, and slowly approached the rusting bus with the broken windows patched with cardboard and the reeking garbage strewn outside, wary for signs of the big black dog.

Twenty yards away the barking began from inside the bus. And at that moment he saw the cat, lying by the side of the rutted track that led to Bundy's place. It was dead, a bullet hole through the side, the lips drawn back from the teeth, the tongue bitten through in the agony of a slow death.

Kitty had been Fran's cat, largely ignoring Judson just as he had ignored the cat. But at the thought of what this discovery would do to Fran he found the cold fury welling inside him. Ignoring the frantic barking he strode up to the bus, kicking a path through the litter of cans, and hammered on the door. "Open up, Bundy, I want to talk to you," he yelled.

The door opened jerkily and Joe Bundy stood on the top step, mother naked except for the greasy red cap that never left his head. The barking inside the bus became more frenzied. "Get away from here before I set the dog on you, McIntyre," he shouted. "I ain't in the mood fer visitors."

"Did you kill that cat?" Judson yelled. "That's Fran's cat, you bastard. She loves that cat."

"I don't know nothin' about no cats. I told you get outa here, McIntyre."

"You ain't fit to live with decent people, Bundy." Judson was practically crying with rage. "Fran cooks these biscuits for you, and you go and kill her cat. What am I going to tell her?"

"Tell her Bundy don't like cats. Nor biscuits." The door rattled shut and Judson heard him inside the bus shouting at the dog to be quiet.

Fran received the news better than Judson expected. But when she said she was going to rest for a while and shut herself in her sewing room he knew she would be crying quietly for a long time. It had happened before when Kitty's mother had been run over by a truck. He wished he knew whether to leave her to her grief or go in and try to comfort her.

It was nearly noon when the barking started. Judson ignored it for a time, but when it became louder he looked out of the window. Killer had come right into the front yard and was standing near the porch. Judson was just about to reach for the saucepan when Fran came out of her sewing room, red eyed but composed.

"Don't chase him away, Judson. He's only an animal, like Kitty. It's not his fault what Joe did."

"Well if you don't take the biscuit, Fran!" Judson shook his head. "I believe you'd ask Bundy in for afternoon tea if he came calling!"

Fran was looking out of the window. "He's stopped barking, Judson. What's that he's got in his mouth?"

Judson stood beside her at the window. "Darned if it don't look like Bundy's filthy old cap. What's he doing with that?"

"There's something strange about him, Judson. I'm

going to let him in."

"You can't let that brute inside the house Fran, if he don't bite you the fleas will. Best let him alone. He'll go away in a few minutes."

"He's trying to tell us something, Judson. Something's happened to Joe. I'm going to open the door."

"Don't you go. I'll do it," Judson said. He went to the front door and opened it a crack, carefully. The dog dropped the cap and retreated to the gate, standing with its legs apart, ready to run.

"He's telling us, Judson. That's why he brought the cap. Something has happened to Joe. Where are my shoes? We'll have to go see."

"For Pete's sake, Fran!" Judson exploded. "The old fool's lying drunk on the floor, that's all you'll find wrong with him. He's just killed your cat. You don't owe him anything."

"You don't have to come, Judson, but if Joe's in trouble I've got to go. That dog's telling us he wants us."

But of course Judson went with her. And of course Fran was right. Joe Bundy was lying at the bottom of the bus steps, still mother naked, snorting in a drunken stupor, but with a jagged piece of bone protruding through the shin of his left leg.

Killer had run home ahead of them. He stood quietly beside Bundy as Fran knelt down amid the garbage. Maybe the brute ain't so vicious after all, Judson thought. He started to move to Fran's side.

The killer lips curled back from killer teeth and a

growl like distant thunder told him he was wrong.

TO SPIKE A GUN

Fran McIntyre was nonplussed. In the forty six years since she had married Judson and moved to the Green House on the Hill in Jackass Creek, she had never faced a problem like this. And she was really upset.

"I don't know what to do," she told Hillis Usry at recess. "One of the girls told me something in strictest confidence, but some something has to be done about it. The poor child needs help."

Hillis Usry was Principal of the four room elementary school that was the heart of Jackass Creek. He knew that of all the parents and grandparents who helped out in the school, Fran was the one the children came to for advice. To most of them she was "Gran," whether they spoke English or Punjabi or came from the Reserve. And if Fran thought a child needed help, there was a good reason for it.

"Sometimes telling a secret is a cry for help," he said. "She evidently needed to tell somebody. If she needs to tell somebody that badly your duty to help her may be more important than keeping your promise."

"I really don't know," Fran said. "Let me think about it till lunch time."

Hillis waited till the four teachers and nine aids and helpers had left the staff room, and phoned the Returning Officer for the area. The Provincial election was scheduled for four days time, and one of the classrooms was being used as the polling station for the village and the outlying farms on the west side of the Fraser. One of the parents was standing for election, a thrill for the village, but Hillis was concerned about the propriety of his demands to use the school for a campaign meeting.

Harvey Kopichek, a large man with an aggressive face, was Fire Chief of the seven man volunteer fire crew, Chairman of the PTA and a pillar of the local church. Hillis considered him a domineering oaf with no manners and an ambition greater than his ability. He had two children at the school, a girl in grade seven who was shy and withdrawn, and a boy in grade five who appeared to be already understudying his father.

Hillis was concerned about the boy. He was a well built lad, bigger than any of his classmates and developing into a bully. Hillis had asked his father to come to the school to discuss the problem, but Kopichek's attitude was that the other kids probably deserved whatever happened to them.

The sun was already hidden by the mountain that rose a thousand feet behind the village when Hillis saw Fran again. Fran had been doing supervision all through the lunch hour, and the children had gone home before she found time to discuss her problem.

"I think I'll have to tell you," she said. "As long as you don't let it go any further I don't think I'm really betraying her confidence. And I hope you'll know what to do."

Hillis put down the books he was marking. "I hope so too," he said. "It sounds bad."

"It is bad. One of the girls is being raped by her father. Once she'd told me she couldn't stop crying, she was in a dreadful state. She doesn't want to go home, but she's scared of what her father will do if she runs away and he catches her. What can we do?"

"There's only one thing we can do," Hillis said. "We can't interfere ourselves. I wish we could take her away from him, but we can't. We've got to report it."

Fran was indignant. "We can't do that! He'll beat her up if he finds out. Or worse. And think of the girl, if it gets known around the village. I promised I wouldn't tell anyone." She dabbed at her eyes.

"Fran, there are two things involved here. One, she wants to end it, and that's why she told you. She's at her wits end and she doesn't know what to do, but she trusts you to find a way out. Two, a teacher is bound by law to report any case of child abuse, sexual or otherwise."

Fran glared at him. "Then I wish I hadn't told you. I'm not a teacher. I don't have to report it. Think of the poor child if the police go round and arrest her father. It would be terrible. All round the village."

"Isn't it terrible already, Fran?" Hillis wondered how he was going to resolve this, how best to explain. "The police won't take action. It'll be a social worker who deals with it. She'll find the girl somewhere safe to live. And then if there's a case, the police can arrest him. Who's the girl?"

"Francie Kopichek. I never could stand that man, and to think he might get elected!"

It couldn't be worse, Hillis thought. Poor little Francie! No wonder she's so withdrawn. I should have been able to see there was something wrong. It's my responsibility to notice the signs. Now, what are we going to do about Kopichek? It's unthinkable to let him get elected to the Legislature. But I can't accuse him of incest just on hearsay. There must by some way to spike his guns. But in just four days?

As far as the children were concerned, Francie had gone to visit relations. The village heard nothing, and Kopichek continued a bombastic election campaign.

And then a logging truck spilled its load on the highway, a motor home went off the road and over the side of the canyon, and the volunteer fire crew were called out to rescue a family of four. But Hillis Usry knew nothing about this, and spent the whole evening brainstorming with his wife in their house with the sloping floors. Shawna was convinced the floors had sloped more since the day they moved in, a not unlikely possibility since the only foundations were railway ties that were being steadily eaten by termites.

The next day Hillis was still agonising over the prospect of an incestuous father in the legislature. He even considered writing a letter to the newspaper. He realised he could be sued if Kopichek were not charged, but even a jail sentence seemed worth it. Until he thought of Shawna.

The motor home was hauled back onto the road, and the owner discovered it had been looted.

Fran McIntyre decided she had to see for herself what sort of family Francie had been sent to, and whether Francie was receiving proper counselling. Against his better judgement, Judson drove her down the canyon highway to Hope.

Fran knocked on the door at the address she had been given. When she returned she reported to Hillis that the people seemed very nice, and Francie was settling in as well as could be expected.

The owner of the motor home gave a list of the stolen items to the police, and a search warrant was issued. The first house to be searched was the Fire Chief's. The police left with several stolen items and Harvey Kopichek in handcuffs.

On election day, Harvey Kopichek's name was not on the ballot.

IT TAKES ONE

No-one ever came knocking at the door in the middle of the night in Jackass Creek. Unless it was an emergency. And there never had been such an emergency as far back as Margaret Davies could remember, ever since she had been growing up in the plywood cabin beside the roundhouse, and certainly not since she had married George Davies and moved with him into the brand new Roadmaster's house with its running water and inside toilet.

Now, the Roadmaster's house was forty one years old. The other houses beside the river had long ago decayed and been demolished, and that meant there were no neighbours to help out in an emergency. If it really was an emergency.

The knocking began again. There certainly was some-one pounding on the front door. Urgently. Or, more accurately, aggressively.

It had to be tonight, Margaret said to no-one in particular as she struggled to fit her feet into the slippers beside the bed. Just when George is away at the convention and I'm all by myself. She shook her head and clucked just as she had clucked at the kindergarten children when she was teaching, but her soft, chubby face had a smile. It always had a smile.

It must be something serious, she thought, the way they're beating on the door. She turned on the light, and hurried through the living room to the kitchen, a galleon under full sail as her white night-dress flowed down from a

135

forty two bust. The front door opened into the lobby off the kitchen, so she went straight to the door and stood on tiptoe to reach for the high bolt.

As she touched the bolt, some inner caution instilled years earlier by her mother made her stop.

"Who is it?"

There was no reply, but the hammering on the door resumed.

"What is it?" Margaret called through the door. "Tell me what you want."

There was a crash, and the door shuddered, and another crash. Terrified, Margaret jumped back and ran into the kitchen. The cable car stopped running an hour ago, so it can't be a drunk from the pub across the river in Stretton, she thought. It could be someone from the party at the Stefaniuk's place, and I'm certainly not letting in a drunk. But then it might be someone bleeding to death and he's just collapsed on the porch.

In Margaret's mind it had to be a he. Even in Jackass Creek women wouldn't go about in the middle of the night collapsing on people's front porches; and anyone collapsing, or for that matter in any kind of difficulty, would have to be bleeding to death.

Perhaps she really should open the door and risk it being a drunk? Better to risk being attacked by a drunk than leave someone bleeding to death in the snow.

But then the attack on the door resumed, and this time the man was shouting, punctuating obscenities with crashes that threatened to rip the bolts right off the flimsy door frame.

"Open up! I know you're in there, you bitch. Open this goddam door or I'll break it down. And don't tell me you're fetching your old man because I know damn well he's out of town. You're alone in there, and I'm comin' in."

Margaret knew the voice instantly. It was Buller Sharman, the drifter from the hobo jungle down on the river bank. Sharman was bad news in Jackass Creek, where for years crime had been an occasional B and E by an illegal immigrant dropping off a freight train or a net set out of season in the river. Sharman had already done time for a rape in the back country, he was suspected of molesting two of the local kindergarten children, and the males of the Jackass Creek religious community were of two minds whether to take him down to the gravel pit and pray over his soul.

One male who had no doubt at all that prayer would be the wrong treatment was Tom Brannigan, the proprietor of the Disaster Site with its three year accumulation of junked cars and empty beer cases that so aggravated his next door neighbour Judson McIntyre.

Brannigan was Jackass Creek's most successful entrepreneur. What he whimsically referred to as his 'franchises' extended from fencing items liberated from apartments in Vancouver to providing the Jackass Creek children and anyone else in need with the drugs of their choice. One of Margaret's many crusades centred on catching Brannigan in the act—dealing, she believed it was called.

He could steal and fence all he wanted as far as she was concerned, but she had spent too many years at Jackass

Creek Elementary School, teaching and caring for two generations of students, to see the present generation slip into Brannigan's clutches. If she had been in the mood to consider the question in the present emergency, it was doubtful who she would have preferred to see escorted away in handcuffs, Tom Brannigan or Buller Sharman.

Tom Brannigan had no such difficulty deciding. His bottom line had recently been seriously affected by the intrusion of Buller Sharman, whose philosophy embraced a concept of sharing the wealth. Other people's wealth. Brannigan would have applauded any activity in the gravel pit on the part of the brethren. Other than prayer.

Margaret Davies, on the other hand, firmly believed that everyone had good in him simply waiting to be encouraged, although the middle of the night hardly seemed an appropriate time.

He doesn't sound as if he's hurt or needing help, she thought, and decided the good in Buller Sharman might well wait till later for encouragement.

She looked quickly round the kitchen to see if there was anything heavy she could move into the lobby in case Sharman broke down the door. There was a high stool on wheels that she used when she did the ironing, but that was too mobile. The only other movable item was the great kitchen table, but she knew that was too heavy for her to drag across the floor.

Margaret was badly frightened, and yet one part of her mind seemed remote, assessing the situation dispassionately. He knows George is away, she thought, so he must want to rape me. A compliment to me, I suppose. He must be drunk! Maybe he has a thing for grey hair. I'm fifty seven years old and I'm not pretty, and I probably weigh a lot more than he does. I'll have to roll on top of him and flatten him.

She began to move into the living room, when the rapping on the window began. He'll break the glass if he goes on like that. And he might cut himself badly, and then he could bleed to death and I'm the only one who can help him. And George will have to go to Hope to get another piece of glass, and glass is so expensive nowadays.

Sharman's heavily bearded face showed like a Halloween horror mask in the light from the kitchen. If I can see him he can see me, Margaret thought, and ran to the light switch. But the bedroom light was still on, a beacon shining through the whole house and into the kitchen. Somehow it seemed important that Sharman should not be able to see her, know which room she was in, what she was doing. She ran through to the bedroom and switched off the light; the sudden darkness was so intense she could feel it pressing comfortingly round her. At least now he won't know where to find me.

The Canadian Pacific diesels throbbing on the nearby tracks seemed louder, the loose windows vibrated in their frames till surely they must crack. The windows! She looked round in renewed panic. Which window was Sharman peering in now? Or was he prowling round the house looking for an open one?

The police! she thought. Call the police, of course, why hadn't she thought of that before? She forced herself to feel her way silently back to the kitchen, where the phone hung on the wall. George had bought a new phone with a memory, and programmed into it the numbers of all the neighbours. Nine-one-one was not a number they had ever used, but he had put that on the first button. As Margaret fumbled for the button, the rapping on the widow began again.

"Fire, police or ambulance?" said a man's voice in her ear.

"Police, please, there's a man trying to break into—"

"Police. Is this an emergency?" cut in a different voice, a woman's voice, pleasant yet somehow not so reassuring.

"Of course it's an emergency!" The panic was rising again. "There's a man trying to break into my house and I'm all alone. Send someone over quickly, I'm in—"

"What is your name, please?" Impersonal, unruffled. And not at all reassuring.

"Margaret Davies." Margaret tried to keep her voice level, but Sharman was at the window and the woman was asking stupid questions.

"Your address?"

"I'm in Jackass Creek, the Old Roadmaster's House by the river, the police all know—"

"I need your actual address, Madam." The voice would brook no argument.

"I don't know the address." Margaret felt as if she was apologizing. "We don't have addresses here, this is Jackass Creek. Just tell them the Old Roadmaster's House, they'll know."

The voice was adamant. "I have to have your actual

street address, Madam. What street do you live in?"

"We call it River Road." Margaret was almost in tears. "But nobody uses that. Tell them it's the road beside the river. Do hurry, please, there's a man outside my house, he's banging on my window, you can hear him."

"River Road? And the number?"

Margaret nearly shouted in her frustration, then remembered Sharman outside. She tried to force all her anger into a furious whisper. "I don't know the number. We don't use numbers here. The police know that. Tell them it's Margaret Davies, the Corporal was in here for coffee yesterday."

The police voice remained calm. And infuriatingly patient. "This is RCMP Divisional Headquarters. There is no-one on duty at night at your local detachment. We shall have to send someone from here, so we must know the address."

Margaret gave way to tears at last. "I just can't tell you the number. I've never bothered to remember it."

"Do you have the number on the front of your house?"

"Yes, it's on the front porch, but—"

"Then turn on the outside light, go and look at the number, and come back and tell me." The voice was talking down to her, treating her like a child.

That was when Margaret lost it. "You stoopid cow!" she hissed. "There's a bloody great brute of a man outside, waiting to rape me." She slammed the phone back on the wall.

The tears were gone. They had been tears of frustra-

141

tion, but the frustration was gone. She wasn't going to argue with a stoopid cow on the end of a telephone. She was on her own, and she was suddenly quite calm. So calm that she found herself wondering about the best way to resist being raped. And then wondering if it would really be so bad after all, now that George's prostate cancer had put an end to any sort of sexual activity in the bedroom. And then wondering what had got into her that she should even entertain such a thought.

Margaret became aware that the telephone was still in her hand. Of course, there were the neighbours. Judson McIntyre would come right away, and so would John Jack. And even Hillis Usry, although Hillis was the school principal and had probably never confronted anyone more dangerous than an irate parent. All the neighbours were on buttons on the phone. But which buttons? Nine-one-one had been easy enough, it was the top button, but there was no special order to the others. All she could do was press any button, and ask whoever answered to alert all the others. She giggled. Sharman would be in for a surprise with angry men advancing from all over the village.

Margaret listened to the ringing tone at the other end of the line.

"What the hell d'you want? You know what time it is?" It was Tom Brannigan's voice, surly as ever, but mercifully he didn't sound drunk.

"I'm sorry to trouble you, Mister Brannigan," Margaret whispered. "I need help. Buller Sharman is trying to break into my house."

The surliness went out of Brannigan's voice like the last dram draining out of a bottle. "Sharman? That bastard? Turn out the lights. Where is he, front or back?"

"He's been at the front mostly, but he keeps staring in the windows."

"You sit tight Mrs. Davies, I'll be right over. You haven't called the cops have you?"

"Well I tried to but the woman was so stupid ..."

"Good, we don't want them. Make sure he can't see you and don't move around. Soon as I get my boots on I'll be right there."

Even Tom Brannigan's a help, Margaret thought, and began to relax, so much that a sudden thought struck her. I hope he's putting on more than his boots. She didn't know whether to giggle or be shocked at herself.

She went back to the bedroom and sat on the bed, proud of her logic. He wouldn't dream of me coming back to bed. He hasn't broken in so far so maybe he doesn't dare make a noise. May as well stay here till Tom Brannigan comes. May as well lie down and relax. I'm not even trembling. George would be proud of me!

An hour passed, or so it seemed. And then there was the crash of a window smashing, and the sound of glass cascading to the kitchen floor. Now George'll have to go and buy another window, was Margaret's first thought; followed immediately by the image of Buller Sharman scrambling through the window and slashing himself to ribbons on the broken shards. It was moments before she realised there had been a sharp cry of pain just as the window smashed. And then there was confused shouting, and yells of pain, and obscenities. Followed by silence.

There was a tapping at the back door, and Brannigan was calling. "It's alright, Mrs. Davies, he's gone. Let me in."

Let Tom Brannigan into my house in the middle of the night and me in my nightdress, what would the neighbours say? I don't trust Brannigan any more than Sharman. But he's never been violent. Not as far as I know. The tapping at the back door became more insistent.

"Are you alright Mrs. Davies? Its Tom Brannigan, let me in."

What would George do? Margaret wondered. But George is a man, it's not the same at all. Oh well! One hand found her robe on the bed beside her. Hurriedly she flung it around herself and instinctively primped her hair. And unbolted the back door.

The dark shape clumped over the step. "You're alright Mrs. Davies?"

"Yes, thank you. I'm a mite shook up though."

"Not surprising. That Sharman's a dangerous bastard. Where's the light switch?'

"Is it safe? Has he gone?" Margaret wondered whether she was more concerned about Sharman or Brannigan. After all, Brannigan had been the focus of her disgust and loathing for months.

"He won't be back. Not for a long time. Let's have some light. Got any coffee going?"

"You haven't hurt him, have you?" Margaret hated even to hurt spiders, which frightened her more even than

Sharman. She switched on the light and led the way into the kitchen.

"Well, not what you'd really call hurt. Sorry about your window, by the way. He had his nose pressed to the window and I had to give him a little tap to get his attention. Must have been a bit harder than I thought."

For the first time, Margaret noticed the baseball bat that Brannigan was leaning against the wall as he sat at the kitchen table.

"His face must be all cut up, then."

"Dunno, it was too dark to see. Shouldn't wonder. Be an improvement anyway."

Margaret busied herself with the coffee maker. Someone had been yelling in pain, yet Brannigan showed no sign of being hurt. She hated the thought of Sharman going back to his shack in the hobo jungle with no-one to look after him.

"How did you manage to chase him away?"

"You wouldn't want to know the details, Mrs. Davies. Just be happy he won't be round the village for a few weeks. He ain't walking so good right now. He may have broke his leg. Maybe a few other things."

Margaret was concerned. "If he's that badly hurt won't he need a doctor?"

"His friends down the jungle can arrange that."

"But won't the police want to know who did it?"

"He won't go to the cops." Brannigan turned to look directly at her. "Anyway, he couldn't prove it was me. And you owe me, so you wouldn't tell. Would you?"

145

Margaret deliberately kept herself busy at the kitchen counter while the coffee brewed. There was something she had to say to Tom Brannigan while she had him in her house, but how to approach it? She had put the sugar on the table and fetched the milk from the fridge and was pouring the coffee before she was ready to attack the matter.

"Mr. Brannigan, I haven't thanked you for coming to my help. I do thank you, and I'm most grateful to you. My husband will want to shake your hand when he comes back. And I suppose I owe you a favour, but I'm going to ask you one instead."

Brannigan sat back in his chair. "Shoot, Mrs. D, anything at all."

"Mr. Brannigan, you've been selling drugs to the children. Don't deny it, I know you have, we all know you have, but we haven't been able to do anything about it. I would happily have had you put behind bars if I could. Don't you make enough money without leading the children astray?"

Brannigan put down his coffee. "That's a pretty strong accusation, Mrs. Davies."

"It's not an accusation, it's simply the truth, and you know it. Now I want you to promise me you won't let those children get near any more drugs."

"Even if what you say was true, and even if I was to agree, how d'you know I'd keep my word?"

"You've shown tonight that you're not all bad, Mr. Brannigan. I think you would. And besides, it wouldn't do to have the police questioning you about who hurt Mr. Sharman, would it? And they might if I told them what happened tonight."

Tom Brannigan looked at her in alarm. "That's blackmail, Mrs. Davies."

Margaret Davies put down her coffee. "That's a pretty strong accusation, Mr. Brannigan."

Slowly a grin spread over Tom Brannigan's face. "Know what, Mrs. Davies," he said admiringly, "You've got the makings of a successful crook."

"Perhaps," said Margaret. "It takes one to know one."

OF FISH AND FOUL

Sophia Regan had been canvassing Jackass Creek all day, on both sides of the CPR tracks. Even an inch and a half of rain as measured in Joe Bundy's slop bucket was unable to damp her determination. She was finding most of the villagers willing enough to sign her petition, so long as she was the one who took the initiative and drove round in the rain. They didn't expect her to achieve anything, particularly since the sawmill across the river in Stretton was owned by the faceless plutocrats of an international giant controlled from overseas. But the company had just laid off all but three of the men in the village and brought in outsiders, so hitting back seemed to be the name of the game. And there was no denying the smoke from the burner was a lot worse than it had been. If anyone could do anything about it, they had to admit, it was Sophia Regan, waspish and abrasive but certainly determined.

"She's an angel," Fran McIntyre would say. But she saw only the best in everyone. "She takes on the causes the rest of us can't be bothered with. She's the one got us the water supply cleaned up, and the sewage system, and gates on the level crossing. But it's a pity she's so overweight, people think twice about inviting her in to sit on their best chairs."

Fran had lived in the village for forty six years. She was there for everyone's troubles. She was the one the charity canvassers went to first. She never turned anyone away, and it was always a good idea to get her name first on the list.

"Woman's like a dose of pox," was Joe Bundy's opinion in a rare sober moment. "Bloody nuisance while you've got her, and damn near impossible to get rid of. Tried to get me banned from the pub, she did. Greyhound ought to ban her from the bus, that backside of hers takes up too many seats."

Old Art Collins was more tolerant, but as a professional hermit even he found visitors a strain on that tolerance. Sophia Regan did to it what seventeen years' wear had done to his bright red Army and Navy suspenders. "Looks just like the Wicked Witch of the West," he would say. "Except for the pointed hat. She sticks that long nose into ever'thing."

Sophia knew Old Art would be a tough nut to crack, so she left the ancient travel trailer with the two flat tires till last as a sort of trophy to be won. If persuasion and argument didn't win Old Art over, she was prepared to stay all evening and ruin the last of the springs on the Lazyboy he had brought back from the dump seven years before.

"We've got to do something about it," Sophia said, repeating her standard preamble. "If we don't start agitating it'll only get worse. They've got to put a proper filter on the burner or else close it down."

Old Art Collins, unabashed in his winter long-johns and five days' stubble, shrugged bony shoulders. "Can't see gettin' signatures on that paper's goin' to do any good." Old Art was in one of his more grouchy moods. He was out of beer and cigarettes and very nearly out of tea, and he was goddamned if he was going to walk a mile and a half and wait in the rain for the cable car across the canyon just to go to the store on a day when building an ark seem like a more profitable occupation. Anyway, one of the few pleasures left in life was having a good reason to be grouchy. Particularly with do-gooders like Sophia Regan. And here she was, beating on the door of his trailer trying to persuade him to sign some stoopid perdition and providing a heaven sent opportunity to unload some of his grouch.

But Sophia knew how to stop a grouch dead in its tracks, even Old Art's grouch. She just talked. And refused to listen. "If you cleaned this place more often you'd see just how much dust and ash there is over everything, all coming from the burner at the mill. There's no reason why they should be allowed to cover us with filth just to save themselves the cost of putting in a proper filter. Do you realise how much pesticide and wood preservative goes up in smoke from the bark and stuff they're burning? That's all in the air you're breathing every day. Look at it out there, right now, all that black smoke. That doesn't stay up there, you know. It all comes down again, all over the countryside. It's washing down in the rain right now, killing the trees and poisoning the people. My Jim's been collecting air samples to send to the Department of Environment, and you should just see what settles to the bottom in those bottles. We're breathing that stuff, getting it into our lungs, and that's only the stuff we can see. Know why we don't see deer and rabbits and racoons and skunks around here anymore? Hardly any squirrels even? The pollution's killed them off. Same with the owls and the hawks. And we're not getting so many swallows as we used to. And there's another thing, see how far up the canyon that black cloud spreads with the wind? They get our pollution all the way up to Lytton. And over in Stretton the high school's right next door to the burner. All the heavy particles fall straight down again over the school, and then they get sucked inside by the air conditioning and circulate round the school. There's been eleven cases of cancer in Stretton in the past five years. I can't prove they've been caused by the mill, but how many of those school kids are going to die in the next twenty years if we don't do something?"

Old Art began to scratch his crotch, caught Sophia's eye and changed his mind. His hand wandered higher till it encountered his scrawny neck. He scratched nervously at the remains of a week old sore and grabbed the pen. But if he thought he was getting rid of Sophia by signing he was very wrong. Sophia Regan had a whole arsenal of iniquities that needed attention. Immediate attention.

"I'm sure you don't smoke marijuana, Mister Collins." She tucked the petition away in the brief case she always carried, and settled back more firmly to punish the last remaining springs in the Lazyboy.

Old Art had opened the door hopefully. He closed it again and breathed heavily. "What's that got to do with the burner at the mill, fer Pete's sake?"

"Nothing at all, Mister Collins. But we have another problem in the village. It concerns that dreadful man Phillips."

"What's the SOB done now?"

Sophia Regan's expressive nose reacted as if confronted by a mouse several months deceased from a surfeit of Limburger cheese. "I'm not sure that I know what an SOB is, Mister Collins. However, the problem is that Mister Phillips has a sizeable marijuana plantation on that land of his outside the village. We have enough of a problem already with the school children getting hold of drugs."

"So tell the Mounties, it's their job."

"And as if that isn't enough, Phillips has put a net out in the swimming hole in Puzy Creek and he's selling the salmon to the tourists."

"Jeez!" Old Art was roused at last. "It's spawning season. Those fish ain't fit to feed the cat on!"

"That doesn't seem to concern Mister Phillips very much. And what about those hovels he rents out in Stretton? They're nothing but fire traps. He's defrauding the Welfare, he turns his cattle loose to feed in the villagers' gardens, he's been in prison for fraud, and he's a generally nasty man. Thank heaven there are a few of us with the guts to do something about it."

Old Art gazed down at the bulk sinking deep into his Lazyboy, and with difficulty kept his thoughts about guts to himself. "Willard Phillips'll run rings round you," he said instead. "Anyway, the villagers are all too scared of Phillips to say boo."

But he had forgotten about Hillis Usry. Hillis was not one of the villagers. Hillis had migrated from the big city five years earlier to steer the Jackass Creek Elementary School through the latest round of government cut-backs, and if he could defy both the Superintendent of Schools and the Chairman of the Board and get away with it, he was certainly not to be intimidated by Willard Phillips.

So it was Hillis Usry who took the cable ferry across the river to Stretton and talked to Corporal Handiside in the RCMP station on the highway. "It's not going to be as easy as you may think," the Head Horseman explained. "Phillips isn't selling the fish himself. He lets his children do it for him, and we can't pull in juveniles for selling fish."

Hillis was incensed. "Can't you catch him hauling in the net? Don't you call it a stake-out or something?"

"I'd like to," Handiside said. "But a stake-out takes men. I've only got three men and one's on leave and one's away sick. If I keep the third man up all night I've no-one for the day shift."

"Well what about the marijuana, then? He can't deny it's on his property."

"But he can deny they're his plants. I'd have to prove he planted them. Or else catch him harvesting them. Believe me, I'm not just being difficult, the drug thing is my biggest problem right now. But I can't be over there waiting for Phillips to start harvesting."

"I can," Hillis said. "How quickly can you get over there if I tip you off?"

"Quick enough," Handiside said. "But I don't want you running into trouble. Phillips may be working with people from down south, and those people play rough."

Hillis grinned. "No trouble. I can see his field from my bedroom window. Between Shawna and me, we'll let you know when it's time to come calling."

And so it was that Willard Phillips had visitors on

the very evening he began to harvest his crop. There were so many plants that Corporal Handiside had to get help from the Lytton detachment. So many, in fact, that he had to borrow a truck from the CPR. So many that he had to use the holding cell to store them and the whole police station began to smell like a pot-house.

"Just as well it's the quiet season," the Corporal said to Hillis after several days with all the windows open. "I've got no place to put the bad guys as long as I have to keep those weeds here."

"How long d'you have to keep it?" Hillis asked.

"Until the Prosecutor's got his paper work done. It's evidence. And it could be a while, because Phillips is hiring a high-priced mouthpiece from the City and he'll be playing all the angles."

It must have been the quiet season in the Prosecutor's office, because within the week word came that the green stuff could be destroyed. Corporal Handiside had fielded the facetious phone calls with good grace, and turned away courteously the jokesters who besieged the police station pleading to be arrested and thrown in the cell for the night. But having to spend so much time in the open air meant the paper work was piling up, so he was relieved when instructions came from Divisional Headquarters to unload his problem in the burner at the mill.

It was a gala day at the mill. Seven constables from Lytton arrived in three police cars, and left their lights flashing. Three top brass and a driver arrived from Headquarters in another car. And left the lights flashing. Two under-cover drug squad with long hair and beery breath drove all the way from Vancouver. In a police car. And left the lights flashing. Sophia Regan insisted on being present to represent the Concerned Citizens of the Canyon. And a multitude of mill employees who seemed not to be employed on anything at all stood behind the yellow crime scene tape and expressed noisy disgust at such a waste of good quality grass.

The performance was over in an hour, and the constables retired to Lytton. The brass retired to Corporal Handiside's office to sample the ambience and commend his vigilance. The undercover men retired to the pub. Sophia Regan crossed one of Willard Phillips' iniquities off her list and phoned the Prosecutor to demand an early trial, reminding him that all the time Phillips was out of jail he was probably raping innocent virgins or selling illegal fish.

When Hillis Usry drove south to attend the monthly principals' meeting at the School Board Office, he was prepared for the usual litany of problems from his opposite number in Stretton's secondary school. Jackson Parker had well above the provincial average of fetal alcohol syndrome children, and far too many who arrived at school with no breakfast inside them.

This time it was a different problem. "They're falling asleep at their desks," Parker reported. "They're never particularly bright in the morning, but by recess they're out to lunch." He smirked self-consciously at the pun. "It's as if they're all on dope."

"You may have hit it," Hillis said thoughtfully, thinking of the rain of fine ash after the gala at the burner.

Two days later the Band Chief reported three dead sturgeon washed up on the sand bar on the east side of the river. "Never seen a dead one before," he said. "You guys been polluting the river again?"

It was Willard Phillips who clinched it. "You assholes!" he yelled, storming into the RCMP station. "How d'you expect me to make a living? I'm trying to live off the land like an honest countryman, and all you can do is take away my livelihood."

"I'm sure we wouldn't want to do that, Mr. Phillips," Corporal Handiside said mildly. "What seems to be the trouble?"

"You know bloody well what the trouble is." Phillips leaned menacingly across the Corporal's desk. "You steal my grass—and my lawyer says you'll have a hard time proving it's mine anyway. And now all my fish are floating belly up, just when the tourists are passing through."

"Illegally caught fish, Mr. Phillips—which I'm sure you'll deny selling because that's illegal too. But how come the fish are dying?"

Phillips pounded the desk with his fist. "As if you didn't know when you burned up three months' work. All that ash. It's still coming down. It's everywhere. It's in the creek and it's collecting in the back eddies and the fish are eating it. It's all over my pasture and the damn cattle have got the staggers. And it's got into the school and my kids came home stoned from school today."

Corporal Handiside smiled gently. "If you'd care to put your complaint in writing, Mister Phillips, we could

156

probably add that to the charge against whoever grew the stuff in the first place."

THE HOUSE

It was not much to write home about. Not that anyone ever would or ever could write home about it. Charlie could no longer see well enough to write; and anyway it happened to be Charlie's home, the only home Charlie had known for the past forty nine years. Before that he had lived in rooms, in cheap hotels, in boarding houses, even in a bordello, always near the railroad tracks, wherever there was work as a fireman and later as an engineer.

To Charlie it was all he wanted, all he had ever needed since he retired to live in the road that ran alongside the tracks he knew so well. In the early days, before he retired, he had looked after his mother and father until one died and the other took to lighting fires in the kitchen sink and had to go to a retirement home. So now there was a spare bedroom upstairs, empty, because no-one ever came to stay. There was a living room where his mother and father gazed down in faded sepia on the electric scooter he could no longer ride and a litter of empty beer cases. There was his bedroom, doorless so that he could keep hold of his walker with both hands and not have to wrestle with a doorknob. There was the kitchen, with a table and chair and rocker and a sink and a fridge and a water heater, and a wood burning range that had come with the house and still served for heating and cooking and burning what little garbage Charlie generated. And there was a cellar, dug out of the ancient river bed boulders three-quarters of a century before, with the shelves still cluttered with forgotten preserves and pickles and bottles of home-brewed beer.

Charlie was still a big man, even though his frame had shrunk with the years. There was no hair left on his head, and the wisps that hung long from his face were so sparse they needed little more than a quick run over with the back side of his electric shaver once every month or so. The dentist had removed the last of his teeth years before, but with his dentures in place his grin was like a pumpkin's at Hallowe'en. At night, when he took them out and put them in the coffee mug beside his bed, his face would shrink till his faded blue eyes seemed to stare out of a living skull.

Charlie's one hundredth birthday had been the biggest event anyone in Jackass Creek could remember. There had been no need to send out invitations. Everyone in the village, and in Stretton on the other side of the Fraser Canyon, had been looking forward to it ever since Charlie's ninetieth, and the bush telegraph had been buzzing east and west along the CPR line for weeks, calling together anyone who had ever fired for Charlie. There was no-one left alive whom Charlie had fired for, because half a century earlier a man had to serve his time as a fireman before he became a driver. The men Charlie had fired for would have been more experienced and older than Charlie. And they were all long gone.

There must have been close to three hundred people in the village hall at Jackass Creek that day. All through the afternoon, there was a group sitting round Charlie, and more hovering near waiting to move in when a place became vacant. All over the hall there was hand-shaking and back-slapping and great shouts of laughter as railroaders recognised faces they had never expected to see again; and wives drew each other aside to leave the men to their stories. Corporal Handiside put on his red serge uniform that had become too tight round the neck, and stood behind Charlie through most of the afternoon so that the Press and the TV and everyone else could take a picture of Charlie with a Mountie.

Tinfish Buckley, who owned the hotel and pub in Stretton, had provided more coffee and tea and milk and soft drinks and sandwiches than everyone could consume. Annie Prendergast had made a cake in the shape of a steam locomotive that everyone said was far too magnificent to be cut into, and they brought it in with one solitary candle marking the century. The piper they had paid to come from Kamloops marched in front, and Charlie interrupted the third telling of the time his train was stuck in a snowdrift outside Yale for five days, to look up and snap in the Yorkshire accent he had never lost, "Sounds to me like someone's stuffed glass up the cat's arse."

It seemed as if Charlie had been hanging on, conserving his strength, determined to make it until that day. Every morning, when Judson McIntyre would drop by to clear the ashes out of the range and bring in the day's wood, the first thing Charlie would say was, "Do you think I'm going to make it to a hundred, Jud?" And Judson would shake his head disgustedly and snap, "Of course, you old devil, you've got a lot of mileage left in you yet."

But, once the great day was past, Charlie seemed to

lose interest. "A hundred's enough fer anyone," he would say. "I'm ready to go. I can't read, I can't walk properly, I can't drink, and I can't screw. Why hang around?"

But he did hang around. The months passed, and getting out of his chair to put another log on the fire became more painful; and climbing in and out of Fran McIntyre's car became impossible, so the weekly trips into town for groceries had to stop. A pleasantly buxom lady from the other side of the tracks appeared and introduced herself as the Home Help, and helped Charlie get out of bed and get dressed every morning, and made sure there was food in the fridge, and came back to put him to bed every night.

Charlie hated it. He hated being dependent on someone else, particularly a woman. He hated the indignity of having a woman helping him off with his long-johns and taking them away to wash them. He hated sitting and dozing in the same chair every day, waiting for some neighbour to drop by. And he hated the terrible fear of stumbling on his way to the bathroom and lying on the hard bare floorboards until someone discovered him.

It was early January in Charlie's hundred and first year that Looey moved into Mabel's House next door. It had been Mabel's House ever since Mabel had been born there to the Roadmaster's wife. That had been back in the prosperous days when Jackass Creek had a passenger station and a hotel and a roundhouse and a post office. Now Mabel was long dead, there were no more passenger trains, and all the other houses beside the tracks had been demolished through the years. But the house next to Charlie's House, the only other house left in the road, was still known as Mabel's House, just as Fran and Judson McIntyre's was the Green House and Joe Bundy's was the School Bus. Because there were no house numbers, or even street names, on that side of the tracks.

When Looey moved into Mabel's House, it had been empty for three weeks. Looey's arrival meant nothing to Charlie. Ever since Willard Phillips had bought Mabel's House for renting out, it had been occupied by a succession of itinerants, none of whom had stayed for long. As far as Charlie was concerned, Looey was just another one in the succession of tenants who might or might not drop in for a chat. He just hoped the latest one hated loud music as much as he did.

And then Looey dropped in for a chat.

"He's a Chinyman!" Charlie protested when Judson arrived the next morning.

"What's wrong with that?" Judson stamped the snow off his boots outside the door, and stacked the firewood he had brought in from the woodpile. "You're a Limey, but we put up with you just the same. We all put our pants on the same way round. Anyway, he's not Chinese, he's from Vietnam."

"He looks like a Chinyman, what's the difference? Furriners. How come you know so much about him, anyway?"

"Fran was getting some groceries over in Stretton, and he was in the store. You know what Fran is when she sees a new face. She asked him to supper tonight, but he wouldn't come. She says he's shy. How come he came to see you?"

"Said he thought it was the thing to do. Said he won't be in again, though. Wants to be alone. Probably to meditate or do yogi or something."

"Better be thankful there'll be no loud music," Judson said. "Seems a cut above the crowd Phillips usually gets. Phillips just bought another broken down place over in Stretton last week. That's three houses here and four in Stretton he's got. Real fire traps, the Stretton ones."

"Bastard was here the other day. Wants to buy this house. Shouting at me, he was. Says I should sign the house over to him. Wants to get the paperwork done before I—"

"What did you tell him?"

"Told him I ain't going fer a long time. Told him anyway I'd burn the place down with me in it before I let him have it. No way is he going to get it. Leaving it to my nephew, it's in my will. My nephew don't need it, but Phillips ain't getting it, that's fer sure."

Judson looked serious. "Watch out for him. He's a devious bastard. He'd swindle the house from over your head and have you out in the road if he could find a way."

Charlie held out an empty mug. "Pour me some coffee before you go. And open the damper a little. The place gets cold when you leave the door open."

"Can't haul in wood without opening the door, you miserable old devil. You going to be alright till this evening?"

"It'll be alright. Miss Piggy comes in at six. Nice cuddly little thing she is. She fancies me. Think I'll haul her into bed."

Judson McIntyre laughed. "You trying to get in the Guinness Book of Records, Charlie? Good thing that pistol's not loaded."

"Fair wore it out when it was, though. Did I ever tell you about the night me and Arthur Phelps stayed the weekend at the whore-house at Lytton?"

"Too many times." Judson opened the door. "See you tomorrow, Charlie."

That morning the Arctic high that had been sleeping all week over Alaska began to wake. And stretch. By nightfall the mercury in the thermometer threatened to freeze and the wind was blasting down from the north like a gale out of the grave. By next morning the weather had the whole of British Columbia firmly in its grip and was heading south into the land of the free.

It was on the second day of the freeze that there was a tap at the kitchen window Charlie always left open enough for Blackie to come and go, and Looey's face appeared shyly over the sill.

"What the hell d'you think you're at?" Charlie snarled. "Can't you come to the door like ordinary people?"

Looey's head bobbed up and down. "No answer at the door. Can I come in, please?"

"If you must. Make sure you close the door after you. Shuttee door. Toot sweet. Savvy?"

If Looey was a Chinyman Charlie knew just how to talk to him. There had been hundreds of Chinese labourers working on the railway in his early days. They spoke no English, but they seemed to understand pidgin if it was shouted at them. Anyway, there was little they needed to understand so long as they did as they were told.

There was a stamping outside the door as Looey kicked off the snow. He came into the kitchen and stood by the door with a large jug in his hand. "Good morning Mister Small. Canyon weather becomes very cold."

"Nothing to what it used to be," Charlie said belligerently. "I've seen it freeze the steam right inside the pistons it was so cold. What you want, eh?"

"If you could let me have some water, please? Nothing coming from my taps."

"Your pipes all froze up? Not surprised. Been no heat in the house fer three weeks. Don't suppose they'll unfreeze till the weather warms. You got a big fire going?"

Looey smiled ruefully. "No fire. Mister Phillips did not tell me he removed all firewood."

"Cheeze!" Charlie exploded, all antagonism to the furriner forgotten. "That SOB would screw his own mother, 'cept he never had no mother. Plenty water here, Looey. Take what you want. Plenty hot water, take that."

"Thank you, Mister Small." Looey moved to the sink. "You can spare hot water?"

"Have to run it off to cool it sometimes. Gets too hot when the fire's going full blast." Charlie had a sudden thought. "You better take some firewood back. Don't suppose you're used to the cold back in Chiney. Pretty hot in Chiney, eh?"

Looey smiled tolerantly. "I come from Vietnam, Mister Small. I've already lived in Vancouver eleven years. Quite used to Canadian climate. But not this much cold."

"That's alright then," Charlie said. "Woodpile's outside. Take what you need."

"Thank you for your kindness, Mister Small. It is nice to have a good neighbour like you. But I think perhaps I shall return to Vancouver tomorrow and stay with friends till the weather improves." Looey gave a little bow before he closed the door behind him.

Seems alright fer a furriner, Charlie thought. Don't seem to have a wife, that's one in his favour. Wonder what he's doing out here in the boonies. Don't seem to have no job to go to.

That afternoon Hillis Usry stopped by on his way home from the Jackass Creek Primary School. "Need anything, Charlie?" he asked cheerfully, putting his head round the door.

"Six foot blonde, but I don't suppose you'd have one of those," Charlie said.

"Not the sort of thing a school principal keeps around the place. Don't think my Shawna would appreciate it either."

"Say, come inside," Charlie said. "I want to ask you something."

Hillis took off his snow boots and closed the door. "What's troubling you, Charlie?"

"Where's Something-Nam? Chinyman next door says he ain't from Chiney. Where's he from?"

"Sounds like Vietnam," Hillis said. "He won't like

being called Chinese if he's from South Vietnam. Does he speak English?"

"Tolerable well. Says he's lived in Vancouver fer eleven years. Not used to this Canyon weather though, I bet."

"Who is? I might ask him to speak to the Grade Sixes. Does he seem friendly?"

"Too damn friendly. Keeps coming in to see me. Doesn't have any water, doesn't have any firewood. That bastard Phillips took all the firewood away."

"I guess you gave him some, did you? Even so he'll be frozen up all winter and he can't live for ever getting water from you. Why don't you let him move in with you?"

"You're out of your mind, Hillis." Charlie was indignant. "I never had no-one live with me since they put the old man away. You know I wouldn't have that. No way I'd have anyone move in here with me. Besides, he's going back down the line tomorrow till it gets warmer."

"Sorry I mentioned it," Hillis said. "Just seemed like a good idea. Well, you need anything just give me a ring. Can you reach the phone alright?"

"It's on the table."

Hillis left, and Charlie replayed their conversation to himself. So the Chinyman wasn't a Chinyman. And Hillis had his nerve, suggesting he should share his place. And with a furriner! And a Chinyman! Even if Hillis said he wasn't one.

That afternoon a warm front passed through and brought the snow. But not ordinary snow. By morning it was coming down in great wet feathery flakes that poured in through Blackie's window and blocked the highway and closed the school and felled the great maple that had been in John Jack's back yard ever since his grandfather's time.

"Over the top of my knee-boots already," Judson MacIntyre reported as he brought in the day's fire logs. "Highway's closed. They say there's more than twenty trucks waiting in Stretton for it to open, and a whole lot more stranded outside of town both ways. Hotel's full right up. Haven't heard any trains come through this morning. Looks like being a bad one, and there's no sign of it letting up. Your Miss Piggy get here this morning alright?"

"She was late. Had to lie in bed till eight o'clock waiting."

"Made you crabby for the rest of the day has it? You're lucky she got here at all. Her old man's got a four-wheel-drive or she wouldn't have made it."

Twenty minutes after Judson left, Looey was at the door. "I was to have returned to Vancouver today but the highway is closed," he said apologetically. "Anyway my car is fully buried in snow. Can I trouble you for more water, please? I must flush the toilet."

"Take what you need," Charlie said. "Don't look like you'll be out of here inside a week. Any other time you could of run a hosepipe across to your place, but she'd freeze in a minute in this weather."

Looey went to the sink to fill his jug, standing as close to the wood-range as he could while still reaching the hot tap.

"Say, you know Hillis Usry?" Charlie said suddenly.

"Principal over at the school."

"I have not had that pleasure," Looey said. "Misses MacIntyre, I think her name is, I met at the general store, and you, but no-one else."

"Wants you to talk to his kids. Says you come from Veet Nam, that right?"

"Yes, South Vietnam. Several years ago. I would be pleased to talk to his children."

"He reckons your pipes'll be froze all winter after the house was empty so long. Guess he's right."

"I shall have to return to Vancouver."

"Not till the road's opened up, you won't."

Looey took his jug of water carefully to the door. Charlie made a sudden decision. He took a deep breath and looked away to the other side of the room. "You want to bunk in here fer a few days that's alright with me. There's a spare bedroom upstairs. Save you hammering on the door every few hours looking fer water. Miss Piggy gets the food and keeps the place clean."

The look of polite deference that had been on Looey's face turned to disbelief, and then to a delighted smile as the tears came into his eyes. He shook his head slowly from side to side, unable to speak.

"No big deal," Charlie said brusquely. "I get people staying here all the time." He grinned. "Women mostly."

Looey brought in his bedding and took it up into the room under the roof, warm in the heat rising up the narrow stairs. Then he went back next door and returned with the supplies he had brought with him from Vancouver. The snow continued to fall through the day, not drifting down in picturesque Christmas card fashion but pouring purposefully and steadily hour after hour. It built up on the kitchen window-sill till the window was opaque. It blanketed every sound from outside the house till they could imagine the world had come to an end. No thundering diesel drowned their conversation; no trucks on the highway the other side of the Fraser shattered the day with their barking engine brakes. Nothing moved.

There was only enough wood in the kitchen to last them through the day. The wood pile would be buried deep, but they must have heat above all. Looey carefully opened the back door, expecting a cascade of snow to fill the hallway. Instead he was faced with a standing wall of snow across the doorway that came up to his thighs.

"Jud leaves the snow shovel leaning against the house outside the door," Charlie said. "Best cut a path to the wood-pile. Little guy like you could disappear without trace in those drifts."

Looey brought in logs, and filled the woodbox, and piled more on the floor in the kitchen until even the freezing pain in his fingers was numbed. And then the one bare bulb that hung from the centre of the ceiling went out.

"Try the phone. See if that's gone off too," Charlie commanded. Looey lifted the phone. The silence was complete.

"No matter," Charlie said. "Takes me back a few years, this does. Back in nineteen ten, or eleven, somewhere about then, me and a couple of wipers from the roundhouse

170

was living in a tent right opposite where the schoolhouse is now. No phone then, no electric. We had a floor of wooden boards, and logs around the sides fer three feet or so, and the rest was canvas. I was still a kid then, so I did the cooking. Lived there fer three years. Every winter it used to snow like this. I remember one day it took me three hours to get from the roundhouse up to the tent, about half a mile I reckon."

Of course there was no Miss Piggy that evening. Looey asked permission to look in the refrigerator and the cupboards in the kitchen, to see what food there was. And stacked away what he had brought. In the freezer compartment he found a heavy package wrapped in brown paper.

"Deer meat," Charlie said. "Been there a while, since Judson went hunting last time. Miss Piggy didn't fancy cooking it. Won't last long now the electric's off."

"Would you like me to cook it for you?" Looey asked.

"You know how?"

"I have cooked many kinds of meat. I will cook it for you tomorrow when it's not frozen."

There was some porridge left over from breakfast in the refrigerator. "Warm that up for me," Charlie said. "Don't look like much, but it's all I can hold down at night. We can have some deer meat for lunch."

Looey warmed up the porridge on the range and poured a glass of milk, and helped Charlie to the kitchen table. When Charlie was finished he prepared something for himself out of a packet.

"That Chinese food?" Charlie asked.

"Vietnamese food."

"Same difference. Don't know how you fellers can stand it. Used to be a bunch of Chinese lived in a shack by the church just over there. Went to play cards with them one evening and they served up some of that stuff. Near made me sick."

It was almost dark by the time Charlie had finished eating. Looey helped him into the bedroom. "Electric blanket won't be working tonight," Charlie said. "You better fill the hot water bottle. It's hanging on the bathroom door."

When Looey returned, Charlie was lying on his back on the bed, cursing. "Fell over," he said. "Once I get on my back I can't get up. Anyway, now you're here, grab these pants and haul them down. Miss Piggy usually has the pleasure. She don't know how lucky she is!"

Looey pulled off the heavy socks and the jeans and the long-johns, and helped him sit up to take off the jacket and sweater.

"Not the undershirt," Charlie barked. "You want me to sleep mother naked? Find me a six foot blonde and maybe I will."

In the morning Looey had coffee made before he heard Charlie calling from his room. "You want me to lie here all day? Miss Piggy usually gets me up at seven-thirty."

Looey took a mug of coffee into the bedroom, and helped Charlie to sit up. "What you like for breakfast?" he asked. "Bacon and eggs?"

"Say, that sounds good!" Charlie grabbed the coffee mug. "I usually have a hard boiled egg and an orange and a piece of toast. Miss Piggy says it's a healthy diet. Some kind of bullshit from the Health Department."

Looey helped him dress, and took him to the bathroom. "You don't want a shower?"

"Shower day's Friday," Charlie said. "Don't need more than one shower in a week."

They were finishing their breakfast when there was a hammering on the door, and Judson McIntyre stamped his way into the kitchen, sou'wester and slicker and hip-waders dripping snow to form pools on the floor. "Cheeze, I've never seen nothing like this before. Must've taken me best part of an hour to get from my house to here. Had to cut a way with a snow shovel to get through it. It's up to my waist. Tried to phone you to see if you were alright but the phones are out."

"Not to worry, Jud. Guess Miss Piggy's snowed in, but Looey's bunking in with me. He ain't got such nice titties but he's doing alright."

"Looey? You the feller's moved into Phillips' place? Fran met you in the store, right?"

Looey smiled and bobbed a bow. "You must be Mister McIntyre. Mister Small says you come in every day and do things for him. No need to worry now. It gives me great pleasure to look after Mister Small. He has been very kind to me."

"How come you want to live up here, Looey, all this way from Vancouver?" When Judson wanted to know something he asked. Tact was not a consideration.

"I like to paint. This is nice country, and I can get away from people."

Judson laughed. "You call bunking with Charlie getting away from people?"

Looey smiled and said nothing.

The snow stopped falling after two days and nights, and the electricity was restored on the third morning. But still the highway remained closed and the rail line remained silent. Looey did everything he could for Charlie throughout that time, eking out their limited rations, stoking the fire every two hours and fetching in more firewood from the buried log pile outside. On the third day, John Jack borrowed a Bobcat and ploughed a trail to Charlie's door. And then Charlie's phone rang. Looey answered the phone.

"Charlie? That doesn't sound like Charlie. Is Charlie alright?"

"Mister Small is fine, thank you," Looey said. "I have been staying with him. Who is this speaking, please?"

"This is Lillian, the Home Help. I've been so worried about Charlie, but I couldn't even get out of the house and the phones were down. Are you sure he's alright?"

"Charlie is very well, thank you, but he looks forward to seeing you again."

"Tell him I'll be round tonight. My husband has a four-wheel drive."

It was four days before the highway was opened to single line traffic, and even then one small convoy was buried by a slide where the road clung to an almost vertical face of the canyon. The first plough came down the railroad tracks from the east, and the sound of diesels was heard once more. Gradually Jackass Creek came back to life.

Judson MacIntyre brought round a gas devil and a propane cylinder, and thawed out Looey's pipes. John Jack cleared the worst of the snow from Looey's car with the Bobcat, and then he and Looey did the rest of the job with shovels. One of the teachers trucked in a half cord of his own firewood and a kerosene heater. And Fran McIntyre sent Judson round with four frozen pies and a tin of muffins.

Looey moved back into the house he rented from Willard Phillips, leaving Charlie to the solitude he had always valued so highly. The landscape was magical in its quilt of white, and Looey's heart soared as he sat at his easel in the upstairs window. But the old man kept returning to his thoughts. Charlie may have preferred to live alone, but he still craved company. He needed an audience for his century of stories. So twice every day Looey put down his brush and trod the path he had cut through the snow to the ancient house with its curling shingles and sloping floors and worn-out linoleum. Sometimes he stayed for an hour. Sometimes in his politeness he could find no way of interrupting the flow and it would be two hours before he could leave, promising faithfully to return. A dingy house, he would say to himself. Not a nice house to live in.

Toward the middle of March, the Home Help found Charlie in a crumpled heap on the floor, his legs tangled with those of his aluminum walker. She guessed he must be dead, but she could not be sure and she called the ambulance station in Stretton. The men all said it was a blessing, because Charlie wanted to go anyway. Fran McIntyre was more upset; she had known Charlie for nearly half a century. But it was

Looey who wept quietly through the night, wept for the old man who had taken him into his house in spite of his dislike for furriners.

Two days later Willard Phillips drove up and parked outside the house he had coveted for so long. There was nothing particularly desirable about the house to make him want it. But the old man had refused him, told him he'd never have it, and that was enough to make up his mind to have it. Anyway, as the owners died or moved away, he would be buying up all the houses that became vacant. Before long he would own all the rental properties in Jackass Creek and Stretton, and then the teachers and the mill-workers and the loggers would pay whatever he decided they should pay if they wanted to live there.

The door would be secured by a padlock, he knew. He had brought a screwdriver to tear the hasp from the frame. He intended to put in a better door anyway, once he took possession. But the padlock was not in its place. He pushed the door open, noticing how it jammed against the tilting floor. The place was warm. In the kitchen the wood range was burning. A table lamp added to the light from the window that looked out onto the bird table. Looey looked up from the table.

"Good afternoon, Mister Phillips," Looey said. "I do not think you knocked."

"What the hell you doin' here?" Phillips was the more truculent for being caught off guard.

"I live here, Mister Phillips."

"The hell you do! This is my place. I'll be buying it

from Charlie's nephew soon as the will goes through. He won't want to keep a shack like this. He'll sell for whatever he can get."

Looey smiled, but it was not his usual politely deferent smile. "I do not think Charlie would like his house to belong to you, Mister Phillips. I have taken steps to make sure that does not happen. I have already arranged to buy the house as soon as the will is probated. It is all in the hands of the lawyer. "I think Charlie would like it better this way."

GINGER

Ben Johansen had never been fond of children while he lived. He preferred cats, and particularly Old Ginger.

There had been five cats on his bed in the cabin among the trees when the Ranger found him. The SPCA had put them down, because nobody wanted a bunch of flea-bitten cats that had belonged to a crazy hermit who chased away kids that threw rocks at his windows. But, in fact, they weren't flea-bitten. Ben had taken care of them, and fed them well, and loved them like—well, family.

It took Ben's spirit three days to get through the Induction process. When he finally arrived, he looked about for his cats, but there were no cats to be seen, in fact no animals of any sort.

"Animals have no place here," They told him. "Animals don't have souls."

"Hell, they're better company than a lot of people," Ben said.

"We don't like that word here," They said sharply. "And you'll have to change your attitude."

When they looked at his file, it showed he'd been honest, generous, god-fearing, caring and kindly. Kindly to animals, anyway. But there were complaints about his attitude toward children. It seemed some parents didn't care what their little angels did, but they didn't think Ben had any right to yell at them. So Ben had to serve a probationary period before they granted him full status. And just to make sure he was going to be able to get along with the junior residents—the real little angels—They assigned him to Children's Care.

Ben was eighty three years old when he died. His neck was skinny and wrinkled and stuck out like a hungry turtle's. His eyes were dark and deep-sunk and he only had two teeth, so his grin was like the front of a Halloween lantern. Most of the angels were a lot younger, those not relaxing in the Geriatric Division. They were able to drift about in their robes with a certain natural grace, whereas Ben insisted on wearing the old mountain boots he'd bought from the Sally Ann and used for nineteen years. Graceful he wasn't. In fact he didn't look like an angel at all, and there was some discussion about whether he was more likely to scare the children to death than comfort them in their final hours. But They remembered the comment in his file about being kindly and caring, and anyway Children's Care was a thousand angels short worldwide that year, so They decided it was worth the risk. It wasn't as if he would actually be visible.

At first, Ben was not very happy. He'd never got along with kids. (The words of the briefing came to him, "Remember, they're children, not kids.") That was until he came across Alice. He'd retreated to the far corner of the ward to stay out of the way of visitors. There were never any visitors near Alice's bed. Alice was not a pretty girl. ("No child is ugly," ran the briefing.) She had a pinched face ravaged by meningitis and sunken, spotty cheeks. And yellow hair that some uncaring hospital aid had sheared to a stubble. She was about nine years old, a tiny, sad, unmoving figure in the great bed.

She stared mutely at Ben with understanding eyes, hazel with wide, black pupils. For the first time in his long, lonely life, Ben fell hopelessly in love.

With a sudden shock he realised that she could see him. And he knew there could be only one reason for that. And then he realised something else. "I don't scare her to death!" he thought, and shut his mind with a snap, because that was a word he mustn't even think. Not just yet, anyway.

He spent every day and every night by her side, leaving her only when They called down to remind him there were other children in his quota needing attention.

"I know what's going to happen to me," she told him. "I'm not frightened. But I'm so very lonely. I don't have anyone to visit me. I don't even have a dolly to hold."

Ben knew all about loneliness. And he knew the cure. But the hospital was full of rules, and one of the rules stated quite bluntly, "PETS ARE NOT ALLOWED."

He called up to Them and pleaded. "This little girl desperately needs a pet. Could you possibly let Old Ginger in, and send him down here as a cat angel? I know he didn't have no soul, but couldn't you bend the rules just this once?"

"Bending the rules is dishonest," They admonished. "That kind of thinking could lead to Consequences."

Ben was distraught. "Hell—er, Heavens, you know as well as I do she's only got three more days. First the hospital rules and now yours. Ain't you s'posed to be merciful or something?"

"You have to learn not to let your emotions get the better of you," They said. "They're clouding your thinking. Have you forgotten you're an angel? You have the power to perform minor miracles, remember."

"I didn't know," Ben said. "I don't think it was in the briefing. What can I do?" But They had switched off.

Ben went to a quiet corner to think. What constituted a minor miracle? What was the difference between a minor miracle and a major miracle? What would happen if he overstepped the bounds and tried to work a major one by mistake?

Someone up there was evidently listening. "It's up to you, Ben," said a quiet, soft voice. "You'll have to decide for yourself. But you can do it if you have the courage. Go for broke, Ben."

Go for broke? That was all very well, but he'd never performed a miracle of any sort before. What would They say if he screwed up? He looked across to the bed where Alice lay, unspeaking, uncomplaining. And heartbreakingly lonely.

Courage? Sure he'd got the courage. He'd go for broke. To hell with Them! If They didn't like it They knew what They could do. They could kick him downstairs if They liked. But first he'd make damn sure Alice had what she needed to make her last three days on earth happy. He closed his eyes tightly and took a deep breath. And thought, "This might be the last breath I ever take as an angel."

"Ginger come to Ben, Ginger!" he called out so loudly he had to open his eyes and look round quickly to see if anyone had heard. But no-one had heard; neither, apparently, had Old Ginger. Ginger had been a big cat, fat round the middle, with big feet and a lion's ruff round his neck. And a tail like a periscope that always stayed up.

And then Ben saw the tail. It was rising from near the pillow on Alice's bed, and there was a great bulge surging under the sheet. He could hear Old Ginger purring, all the way across the room. He heard something else, too, a delighted chuckle that came from the bed. And for the first time Ben saw her smile.